TARGETING

MEDIA

RELATIONS

About the Author

David Wragg was formerly Head of Corporate Communications for the Royal Bank of Scotland. A former journalist, he has worked in public relations since 1974 and has covered such diverse sectors as transport, energy, the manufacturing industry and financial services. A member of the Institute of Public Relations, he is the author of *The Public Relations Handbook* (Basil Blackwell, 1992), *Public Relations for Sales and Marketing Management* (Kogan Page, 1987 (paperback edition, 1992)), which has also been translated into Spanish and Portuguese, and *Publicity and Customer Relations in Transport Management* (Gower, 1982). He also contributes the public relations chapters for the *Gower Handbook of Management*, the third edition of which was published in spring 1992.

TARGETING

MEDIA

RELATIONS

A Step-by-Step Guide to
Cost-Effective
Public Relations

D A V I D   W R A G G

KOGAN
PAGE

For my wife, Ann

Kogan Page Limited
120 Pentonville Road
London N1 9JN

© David Wragg 1993

British Library Cataloguing in Publication Data

A CIP record for this book is available from the British Library.

ISBN 0 7494 0825 1

Typeset by DP Photosetting, Aylesbury, Bucks
Printed and bound in Great Britain by
Biddles Ltd., Guildford and King's Lynn.

Contents

1
Public Relations as a Precise Tool

Public relations, of which media relations is just one aspect, is often derided as an imprecise tool. The appeal which public relations maintains for marketing specialists and for general management, not just in business but in many other types of organization as well, is that of its perceived cheapness. Clients or employers of public relations services view media relations as being inexpensive because of the free newspaper and magazine space, and free air time, to which media relations provides access. Users of media relations consider the often heavy costs of advertising, and make comparisons with the free editorial space which can be made available.

The truth is that public relations is no more or less easy to target than any other aspect of communication or promotion. Advertising can be carefully and accurately targeted, but one can also cite examples of advertising which falls wide of the mark, either because it appears in the wrong place due to faulty media planning and buying, or because poor creativity, or an over-indulgent excess of creativity, ensures that the all-important message is not conveyed to the target audience. Sometimes, an advertisement, or even an entire campaign, can be afflicted by both of these problems, so that poor media selection and misdirected creativity combine to waste the client's money.

To digress slightly, sponsorship, which is sometimes an element of public relations, but more usually belongs to marketing, is another activity which can be precise, or which can fail to deliver any benefits to the sponsor. Examples of good sponsorship abound. Cornhill Assurance's sponsorship of cricket was instrumental in raising the company's profile with the target audience for its products. On the other hand, many companies sponsor because they believe that they should do something, or because of who they are or where they are based, and ignore the benefits. For some, sponsorship is a means of achieving a corporate entertainment facility, but because they are labelled as the sponsors, the benefits are obtained at far too high a price and could be obtained less expensively if a more professional approach were taken.

Sometimes, the poor impact of sponsorship is a direct result of managements sponsoring activities which appeal to them, rather than to their customers. One building society chairman sponsored a society for a particular breed of cattle, even though his organization was not involved in providing agricultural mortgages: The reason was, of course, that breeding this particular animal was his own hobby!

Of course, sponsorship is one activity which requires additional support from advertising and media relations if the full benefits are to be obtained in the sense of improved image and visibility of the sponsor.

Apart from the perceived lack of precision, there is another obstacle to improving the targeting of media relations. The problem is that many managements do not know why media relations is important, still less what they can ask of the media relations team. There are two different aspects to this. One is the management team who see the role of media relations as obtaining coverage in their own trade or professional media, in effect telling their peer group how clever they are, but unfortunately failing to attract the attention of customers, distributors, suppliers or investors. The other problem is the manager who believes that he or she either should not pronounce on an issue, or who believes that no one will be interested in what he or she has to say. Such modesty is not disarming, but instead is a lost opportunity when a concise, relevant, well-timed and well-targeted message from someone of standing in a particular industry will be of interest to the media.

MEDIA RELATIONS AS A PRECISE TOOL

Having condemned poor targeting in advertising and sponsorship, it is time to put our own house in order and have our attention turned to the defects in much media relations activity. It does help if one is fully aware of the situation at the outset, and can appreciate the way in which the organization, its products or activities, and its media relations are perceived by the main target audiences and, of course, by the press and broadcasters.

Nevertheless, since this also has a bearing on assessing t
of media relations programmes, the question of ass
results is left to near the end of this book in Chapter 13.

Media relations is important not just because it is a core activity
in any public relations function, but because the media act as a
conduit to those other audiences which are so important to an
organization. This is also the reason for media relations having a
bearing on many other aspects of public relations activity, as we
will see in the next chapter.

Reaching the right audience

The media are in fact 'opinion formers'. This accolade is not
confined to the select few who grace television programmes with
their presence, but can be applied to a substantial proportion of
those working in journalism. A criticism of a company or
government policy may sway the reader or listener, although, of
course, some will regard this as biased reporting, and others will
reject it because of their own political inclinations. Nevertheless, a
criticism of a new product or a service provided by an organization,
is less likely to be mitigated by any audience perceptions of bias! A
new car or a new building is either all that it claims to be, or it isn't,
and, equally there is little scope for subjective assessments in
evaluating many products. Praise in the columns of a newspaper, or
on the air, for a new product or service, or for the way in which the
management of an organization has tackled a difficult situation,
will also do much to influence public opinion. Such praise does not
have to be on the front page of *The Times*; it might do just as much
good, if not more, if it impresses the right target audience by
appearing on the inside pages of a local weekly newspaper or a
respected trade or professional journal.

This is why reaching the right media for the story and for the
audience is so important and can be so worthwhile both in terms of
improved sales and image. It might also do much for the share
price, which is another significant consideration for any company
wishing to maintain its independence. Yet, to be absolutely frank,
much media relations activity is poorly planned and poorly, if not
wrongly, executed.

In considering the targeting of media relations, one is not
demanding that only those interested in a story get to know about
it. It is impossible for any widespread communication to achieve
this. After all, when one passes the venue for a major sponsored

event, one cannot help noticing the sponsor's name on the posters outside, but one is not necessarily interested in the activity, the sponsor or the products which the sponsor offers. The same is true of advertising. Leafing through the pages of a colour supplement, every reader is unlikely to be interested in everything on offer!

The media relations equivalent of these examples is not hard to find. A newspaper might contain features on motoring and gardening each week, but it does not necessarily follow that every reader is interested in these activities. This is the difference between the general media and the specialized. The story has to be more interesting for a wider audience for the general press to take it, and the value lies in the fact that it then reaches an audience much of which is interested, but not so committed to the activity that it takes specialized publications. Even those who are mildly interested in motoring buy motor cars!

Faults in media relations

On the other hand, there are few journalists who do not have stories of their daily mail bag containing material which is wildly irrelevant. It might be hard to believe but is nonetheless true that radio stations do receive photographs with press releases, and that learned professional journals are sent new product stories when the editor is only interested in publishing academic papers!

These examples are not exaggerated. One small group of companies engaged in financial services, including leasing and factoring, had public relations proposals prepared by a major London PR consultancy. The consultant handling the account admitted afterwards that the use of a word processor had meant that five similar proposals had been prepared, with only certain names changed. This ignored substantial differences in the businesses concerned, with activities as varied as factoring, leasing and credit cards, and differences in the scale of the individual projects which they handled. Worse still, the media distribution list for each company had been prepared without thought for the business activity or for the publications listed. One company dealing in major leasing business, 'big ticket' leasing in the trade jargon, had magazines for aircraft enthusiasts listed. Another, dealing with smaller projects such as commercial and local authority vehicles, found its media list to include publications aimed at vintage vehicle enthusiasts!

The PR consultancy did not obtain the business for this particular group, and soon afterwards lost the business of the parent group as well.

On arrival in a new post, the incoming public relations chief will often find horror stories in the media relations activity. On arrival in one financial institution, the author discovered that some two-thirds of the media distribution list was out-of-date, including among other examples, an independent television station which had ceased to exist some three or four years previously when the franchise had been awarded to another company.

In another post with a different financial institution, financial and personal finance journalists were found to be on the same list, irrespective of different interests. The same list included many local newspaper journalists who received the same press releases as their counterparts on national newspapers, regardless of the relevance. Indeed, the use of a single, all-embracing media or press distribution list is the source of much poor targeting.

Participating in a training seminar for young press officers at the Royal Bank of Scotland, the Chief Press Officer, the redoubtable Alwyn James, asked the business and finance section of the *Scotsman* if he could have the discarded envelopes from just one morning's post so that he could show the press officers both the volume of material reaching just one department on a daily newspaper, and the extent to which much of it was wrongly addressed. The discarded envelopes filled a large dustbin liner, while the extent to which the envelopes were wrongly addressed exceeded all expectations. There were many addressed to journalists who had left some years previously, and indeed, even to their predecessors. A number of envelopes were also addressed to journalists who had died. Obviously, many organizations suffered from mailing lists five or more years out-of-date.

Even the editors of employee newspapers or magazines will find that their daily mail includes press releases for products unlikely to be of interest to their readers. Indeed, most employee communications do not run stories on products other than those of their own company, and the only occasion when this unwritten rule is breached arises when a product is offered as a competition prize for the readers. Put quite simply, employee communications are about an organization and those working for it, and seek to avoid repeating the type of material which can be found in the general media.

The reason why so much media relations activity is wasted is that there is little attempt to 'think through' the activity. Leaving aside poorly drafted media releases, major faults in much media relations activity include:

- Limiting the activity to client or employer expectations, which might be more concerned with peer group recognition than effective communication.

- Failing to consider the real audience for the message; is it the customers, the distributors or agents, investors, or the community?

- Ignoring, or simply failing to recognize, seasonal opportunities.

- Overlooking other special opportunities brought about by external developments, such as proposed legislation, for example.

- Forgetting the general media at times when a story could be of interest to them.

- Ignoring deadlines, or forgetting the differences in deadlines for different publications.

- Forgetting local and regional media, including the 2100 local and regional newspapers, many of which are better read than the national dailies.

- Not taking the specialized press into consideration, including trade, technical and professional magazines, and those dealing with interests or hobbies, or reaching ethnic and other groups.

- Failing to keep media distribution lists up-to-date.

An example of the temptation of simply confining media relations activity to the expectations of an employer or client was apparent to the author in the case of a manufacturer, Twinlock, of which more in Chapter 4.

The reason so many critics of media relations activity in marketing and, indeed, in other management disciplines, still accept the activity is that, in their view, the value of media relations lies in the low cost of PR-generated media coverage. The more thoughtful might also suggest that media relations offers the advantage that it is more likely to be noticed by the public, or other target audiences, than advertising or other promotional activity. This is because most people do not buy newspapers or tune into the radio or television for the advertisements, but instead are looking for news, features or entertainment.

Handled well, media relations can be as precise as advertising in reaching the targeted audience, far more persuasive and, as a result, far more cost-effective. This means finding and using high quality professionals. While one hopes that when media relations falls to a team rather than one individual, some members of the team will be at an earlier stage of their career and receiving sound advice and guidance, this can only be done in a professional environment and using too high a proportion of inexperienced staff contributes to the problems of providing effective and credible media relations.

We will see in Chapter 3 just how diverse the media can be in the United Kingdom, and this diversity is echoed in many other countries. In some countries, the media is more likely to be regionalized, while in the UK, there is a strong national press as well.

One should not become so focussed on media relations that one ignores the advantages of other means of promotion. For the media relations specialist, a poor awareness of the other forms of promotion and too much emphasis on media relations as the cost-effective solution to all problems, will carry the danger that clients and employers have their expectations raised too high, and meeting such expectations becomes impossible. There are limitations for media relations as for any other activity. A product which has changed little over the years will have scant news value, and will usually have to rely on advertising. If one knows one's customers well, and they are likely to be interested in repeat purchases or open to the idea of buying other products, then using direct mail will be a more attractive proposition. On the other hand, if a company cannot advertise tobacco products on television, for example, it can sponsor sporting events instead. There are occasions when one has to look at the overall balance and impact of public relations and marketing, rather than be too concerned about which compartment a particular activity belongs to.

Anyone who has moved between organizations will have stories of opportunities missed because of poor targeting and poor coordination of effort. One can argue that this boils down to one failing on the part of those concerned, laziness. Nevertheless, organizations are often guilty of encouraging this by stressing the wrong aspect of media relations.

Poor press releases

Another major fault with many organizations is that they take the 'salesman's approach' to press releases, believing that a press release should be like a crowded shop window, with every item mentioned. It is important, when promoting several products, to separate them unless they genuinely are part of a common package. Financial institutions might be offering several new investment products, for example, but the audience for, say, a unit trust, a specialized pension scheme for directors, a school fees plan and an endowment savings plan will be completely different, and so too will the appropriate media. The personal finance journalists will be interested, of course, but might want the products to appear in different articles or columns within an appropriate section, but one will also have to reach publications which might be read by directors or their financial advisers, and reach journalists writing on education. That apart, offering all four products together in a single press release will confuse journalists, and the release itself will be too long to be easily and quickly digested.

The difficulties encountered when media relations is influenced by those who believe that every conceivable feature of a new product should be mentioned has its parallel with those who confuse the purely informational role of media relations with a legal contract. How many well-drafted press releases have suffered at the hands of those who see a legal problem in every phrase? Press releases must be honest and must never be misleading, but they are there to attract the attention of journalists who will take from the story that which they consider to be newsworthy and of interest to their readers or listeners. Too much detail will kill the story by drowning the basic message, and too many preconditions and let-out clauses will confuse and so dilute the impact, that the story will simply never see the light of day.

From the point of view of the potential customer, a press release only surfaces as a news story, and the role of the story is to inform, and to encourage those whose interest is aroused to find out more about it for themselves.

DEFINING TARGETS

Targeting is important, to avoid waste and, still more important, to avoid irritating journalists so much that, whenever a story, suitable or otherwise, is sent to them, it is consigned automatically to the waste paper bin. To ignore targeting a story is to miss an opportunity. Examples of poorly constructed media distribution lists, the first principle in targeting material, abound. The examples of the financial institutions and the poor or outdated media distribution lists are, sadly, not untypical.

There are many different ways to approach the problem, or perhaps one should say the opportunity, of targeting, and these include:

1. Assessing the audience:
    (a) Is it internal or external?
    (b) If the former, does it comprise everyone in the organization, or is it divided by skill grouping, seniority, or location?
    (c) In the case of an external audience, can it be divided in any way, and perhaps separated out from the mass of the population as a whole?
2. What are the characteristics of the audience, and what interests them?
3. Looking at the media available, what kind of material do they handle, and which journalists aim for your particular target audience?
4. Is there a local angle which will make the story of more interest to the media in a particular part of the country?
5. Is the message visual, so that a photograph will catch the eye?
6. What other activities, such as sponsorship, will attract the attention of the audience?
7. Is it possible to approach the audience direct, perhaps writing a letter or using direct mail?

There are many ways of drawing one's organization to the attention of a specific audience. When Cornhill, the major insurance company, sponsored cricket test matches, their research showed that audience awareness of the company had increased more than tenfold over the period of the sponsorship. The only problem was that the enhanced awareness was among those interested in cricket, but since this could be taken as a worthwhile target audience for life assurance products, then all was well. Of course, if an even wider audience had been sought, then the operation would have been just partially successful.

A certain level of public awareness of an organization is often an essential prerequisite for sponsorship. Some years ago, an

American airline, Braniff, sponsored a tennis tournament and the author recalls several people asking 'who or what is Braniff?' They were surprised to discover that this was a major American airline which had just commenced a service to the UK.

Targeting methods

Every story should have more than one angle. A new senior appointment will be of interest to your organization's business or professional press, but in addition it will be of value in the home town of the individual concerned, and at the location where he or she is likely to be based.

A new product will be of interest to the appropriate specialized media, but in some cases, it might be of interest to a wider press. A significant new invention might be of interest to the national media, as well as to the appropriate trade or business publications, but even consumer products have their own particular slots. Many newspapers and magazines run articles or features on new products, of which the most popular are probably the motoring columns, but there are also special features on gardening, home improvements and travel, as well as on financial products. Some stories can also be of interest to the local and regional media, especially if there is a local angle, perhaps with the story quoting the local manager instead of someone at a far-away head office. Even so, in the latter case, it would be a mistake to overlook the financial services media.

The problem is that far too many public relations practitioners fail to understand the media available to them, or the market for the product, let alone the audience for the message.

It is also important never to forget or overlook the seasonal opportunity. The most obvious of these must be the Christmas market, for which magazines and newspapers will include gift ideas or ideas for entertaining. This important aspect of media relations is covered more fully in Chapter 6. One problem with seasonal features is that they are often prepared months in advance. Even newspapers will often have their personal finance columns written by Wednesday for the following Sunday.

Of course, there is one simple question to ask yourself when considering this all-important question of targeting your PR activity, and that is, why am I doing this?

CHECKLIST

- When did you last review your media list or lists?

- Are the media for all of your organization's target audiences represented on your media lists?

- Are the media for all of your organization's different activities or products covered by the distribution lists?

- Do your lists include media for each of your main locations?

2
The Role of Public Relations

Before looking at media relations further, it is helpful to consider the wider picture, and deal with the role of public relations. It is important to understand exactly what is and what isn't covered by the broad catch-all title, public relations, if only because few professions are so widely misunderstood.

The difficulty arises not so often because people admit to misunderstanding public relations, but instead, rather the reverse. One can after all, frequently hear of certain activities or events being described as 'good' or 'bad' pieces of public relations. While one has to accept that relationships with the public will often be influenced for better or for worse by the actions and attitudes of sometimes fairly junior employees who have public contact, their role cannot be regarded as being part of any formal public relations function. Examples of this abound, and include shop assistants, switchboard operators, workers in public transport or for local authorities and public utilities.

Further confusion is created by the variety of terms used by different organizations to describe their public relations activity. The author, for example, has worked in an Information and Public Relations Department, which was part of an International Relations Division; then in an Information Section; in a Group Public Relations function, and in a Press and Public Relations Department, which had only just changed from being Press and Information...; before moving to a Group Corporate Communications Department. A quick look at the recruitment pages of the general press will soon show that vacancies with 'information' in the title could equally relate to computer systems or management or accountancy services roles. The term 'communications' in major corporations will often relate to the provision of telecommunications and perhaps postal or messenger services.

Apart from the titles mentioned, public relations functions will sometimes be graced with terms such as 'corporate affairs', 'public affairs', 'external affairs' or 'external relations', and variations upon these themes. In the United Kingdom, government departments like to use the term 'information division', or department, with the people working being information officers, and so on. One will also come across some specialized terminology, such as 'press secretary'. These terms are rather better, as we will see, than the use of the word 'publicity', and far better than hiding 'PR' in an advertising or marketing department.

DEFINING PUBLIC RELATIONS

Despite this abundance of titles, is it possible to arrive at a respectable and workable definition?

There are indeed several definitions of public relations. The best, and that favoured by the Institute of Public Relations, is that it is the application of a planned and sustained programme of communications between an organization and those audiences essential to its success. There are some variations on this definition, most usually in those cases in which the term 'audiences' is replaced by the alternative 'publics', which is a far uglier term, better suited to bars and conveniences! On the other hand, marketing people might prefer to use the term 'markets', and while this is not quite the same as audiences, there can be occasions when the two are synonymous.

The official definition is, to some extent, incomplete. After all, we need to consider the way in which advertising, marketing and public relations relate to one another, but often PR will exclude advertising. Indeed, there are those who suggest that the difference between the two is that, with advertising, the organization can pay for the space or the air time, and within reason, say what it wishes. With public relations, the space or air time is free, and although it is true that control over the message is limited, the message will still be more likely to attract the attention of the audience. In this definition, one really should substitute the term 'media relations' for the wider and more general 'public relations'. Many will still use the term 'press relations' than the more accurate, and up-to-date, media relations, but this is the least of our problems. Media relations is one of the most important aspects of public relations, but it is not the only aspect. It is important because the media often become the primary channel of communication to the audience or audiences, and play a significant role in forming the opinions of target audiences.

In effect, the difference is that public relations will often be more subtle than advertising, capitalizing on certain strengths at specific times. Public relations will exploit news or features value, while advertising will ensure consistent product or brand support. While a lengthy message might not work in an advertisement, it might well be more palatable as a feature in a quality newspaper or trade and professional journal. The indirectness of PR might mean a background story on a new development or a major personality, while advertising will concentrate more on products or companies. The lengthy background feature is an important aspect of media relations but such features can appear only in certain types of publication, and not only would such a feature be rejected by the popular press, it would have little or no impact on their readers even if it did appear.

Just as advertising means more than press advertising, or even radio and television commercials, PR means more than media relations, and can embrace many internal and external communications, as well as activities such as conferences or sponsorship, for example.

There will be occasions when public relations practitioners will resort to advertising, as we will see later, while one also has to take into account 'advertorials', which are an uneasy, but occasionally useful, hybrid between public relations and advertising in some trade and many local newspapers.

A major advantage of public relations techniques is that they are generally, and usually rightly, regarded as being cost-effective, with a well-managed public relations campaign often having greater impact than advertising, yet at a fraction of the cost. The precondition has to be that such campaigns must be well managed, and indeed, there must also be scope in the subject matter for PR to work. Media relations in particular, while cost-effective, do require substance. The more serious the medium, the less interested the editorial staff will be in gimmicks or lightly-constructed stories. The truth is that the so-called 'PR puff' is blatantly obvious to many journalists, and to their readers, listeners or viewers.

One should be wary of easy descriptions, such as those which infer that marketing and public relations are one and the same thing, when in fact they are overlapping disciplines but with a substantial area of difference. It is somewhat on a parallel with the often pronounced doctrine that a government's defence policy is a tool of foreign policy and should be fashioned solely by foreign policy or diplomatic considerations. This overlooks the fact that the armed forces will also be concerned, in the UK at least, with such matters as fisheries protection, rescue services, and internal security, as well as other occasional activities in aid of the civil power. In the same way, public relations activity will be influenced by such matters as personnel policy, relationships with investors and the stock markets, as well as wider community relations considerations and political liaison, even if we are considering a truly commercial organization.

WHY PUBLIC RELATIONS?

Media relations should be set against the wider role of public relations as a whole. Like it or not, all organizations have a need to communicate, simply because they are part of the world around them and do not operate in a vacuum. Organizations of any size have no choice, they must communicate. It is not simply a question of promoting the organization, gaining more sales or ensuring that a charitable appeal, to take another example, is well supported, it is often a case of defending and justifying a course of action. Pressure groups are other major users of media relations, appreciating perhaps more than many commercial concerns just how important good media relations can be in furthering their aims.

To take a negative view for a moment, one has to accept that all organizations are prone to be misunderstood. Not only does everyone believe that they can run the organization better than the professionals entrusted with its development, but the problems of business and government are widely misunderstood and often misrepresented. Pressure groups, political parties and unions, amongst others, will often be anxious to infer irresponsibility, short-sightedness or a preoccupation with profits in the case of a business. Charities and other non-commercial organizations have this same need to justify their actions.

The consequences of ignoring the wider community relations issues, for example, can be considerable. As an example, a retailer might find that deliveries are difficult and costly because of restrictions on heavy lorries imposed by a local authority which has bowed to local amenity groups, and neither the local authority itself nor the amenity groups might have appreciated the implications for business and the overall prosperity of the area fully. A government could lose an election because its policies were not explained properly and the reasons behind them were misunderstood by the electorate. These two examples might seem too esoteric for the smaller businessman struggling to keep his customers and employees happy, while coping with the problems of intensive competition, rising costs, exchange rate fluctuations and high interest rates, but he will also find that public relations can assist in communicating with customers, employees, the local community, the providers of finance, and so on, and in each case PR should embrace existing and prospective employees, customers, suppliers or investors.

Public relations is sometimes dismissed as 'propaganda' by the more cynical, but there is a vast difference between public relations activity and propaganda. At best, the propagandist will be purely concerned about the good side of the story, concealing and even denying the existence of unpalatable facts, and at worst propaganda is likely to include half-truths and lies, and may well extend to unfair and ill-founded criticism of rivals or competitors. Such activities have no place in public relations, and would be regarded by respectable public relations practitioners, regardless of whether they are consultants or employed 'in-house', as being unethical.

By contrast, public relations is more concerned about communication with audiences. It will entail facing up to problems and explaining the background to these, endeavouring to obtain sympathy and understanding through an appreciation of the difficulties facing an organization and an understanding of what can be done to resolve problems. It will highlight the good about an organization, but it will do so truthfully and factually. Ideally, communication will be two-way, so that the audience perceptions of the organization are understood, and responded to.

It follows that credibility is an important element in any public relations programme. Organizations which are badly, or dishonestly managed, have difficulty in sustaining a credible public relations campaign. One cannot handle public relations for a poor product or an appalling organization, and certainly not for an organization which has problems which it either fails to recognize or which it has no intention of redressing.

Defining the audience

Audiences are sometimes divided into four different categories, or, to use the jargon, 'publics'. These are generally taken as being:

1. Functional publics – these enable the organization to perform its chosen task, and will include customers, whether these are consumers or other businesses, employees and the trade unions which represent them, and suppliers of raw materials and components, or, in the case of a retailer, of the goods which are being sold.

2. Enabling publics – while this description might seem similar to that of the functional publics, enabling publics are those which permit the organization to function within the framework of the society to which it belongs, including regulatory bodies, community leaders, politicians, and shareholders.

3. Diffused publics – this term is used to describe the media, pressure groups and local residents, largely because these are varied audiences and often, in the case of pressure groups and the media, avenues to other major audiences.

4. Normative publics – this term is most often applied to trade associations and professional bodies, but can also include political parties.

Clearly, there is considerable overlap between these 'publics', since political parties, pressure groups and politicians can include many of the same people, and these might also be consumers or employees. One of the major challenges for any public relations campaign is that of ensuring that the appropriate message reaches the right audience, that is, the problem of targeting the message. This is not to say that one looks for different messages for different audiences, since a certain consistency has to be maintained, but rather that the emphasis might be different. This is not difficult to understand, since in any new development, the consumer will want to know about the product developments, the employees about job security and opportunities for advancement, the shareholders about profits, and there may also be questions about the impact, if any, on the environment, for example. It can be that different audiences have similar interests; for example, a politician might be interested in the impact on employees or on job prospects, as well as environmental considerations.

This variety of audiences and the spread of public relations gives some idea of the complexity of the subject. People living close to a major factory will be as much interested in the impact of new products on employment, and hence the standard of living and prosperity of the community dependent on the factory, as they will in any product features or advantages.

ASPECTS OF PUBLIC RELATIONS

Now that we have some idea as to what public relations is, and why it is so important, we ought to look at the different aspects of public relations activity which, combined, can add up to a complete programme. These main elements which constitute public relations activity will include the following:

1. Media relations – still often referred to as press relations, but the new title is more accurate and reflects the importance of broadcasting, including such media as Ceefax, Teletext and other screen-based information systems.

2. Employee communications – employees constitute an important audience for any organization, regardless of its activity, and while this is sometimes disguised in such titles as internal communications or staff communications, the fact is that even senior managers, and sometimes directors, are employees of an organization.

3. Investor relations – most obviously for publicly quoted companies, investor relations is sometimes viewed as consisting purely and simply of a glossy report and accounts, but in fact it goes far further, including announcements to the stock exchanges on which the business might be quoted, and with such matters as briefing of investment analysts and institutional investors.

4. Political relations – organizations, whether their activity is commercial, charitable, political, or whatever, will also depend heavily on good relations with politicians and their advisers, although in many industries, this responsibility is left to trade associations.

5. Corporate identity – corporate identity or image issues have been much to the fore in recent years, but these relate to more

than just a bright and glossy logo, notably to the way in which the organization relates to its constituent parts.

6. Sponsorship – public relations activity will often embrace sponsorship, not because of any desire to cheat the marketing department of this, but because sponsorship activity might not necessarily be in pursuit of marketing objectives, but instead be for community, investment or political reasons, or even because it includes the chairman's favourite hobby.

7. Community relations – this covers a wide spread of activity, including contact with pressure groups or important potential target audiences, such as school children or students.

8. Customer relations – good relationships with customers might be the responsibility of the sales or marketing departments, but input from the public relations function will often be inevitable.

Not every organization will require the full range of public relations techniques, while PR people, especially those working for larger organizations or in more junior roles, will often find that they specialize. This tendency to specialization also follows later in the career of a PR practitioner, since, for example, investor relations will require a high level of skill and experience, as well as considerable mental sharpness.

Media relations has an important role to play in several of the other aspects of public relations, not simply abutting onto these activities, but often performing a major role in the way in which employee communications, investor relations, sponsorship and community or customer relations function. This is not because organizations expect to conduct their employee communications through the general news media, for example, but because employees and prospective employees will also respond to the news about the organization in the general media. A company which is well perceived by the general media and well reported by them will often be a more attractive proposition for prospective employees. Existing employees can have their morale boosted by good reports of their company; after all, people enjoy being associated with success. Sadly, the opposite is true, and employees whose morale might be poor will be depressed still further if their employer is presented as an organization failing to achieve its potential.

In the case of investor relations, investors will be interested in media reports of the company, particularly because it is the practice of many financial writers to seek the views of investment analysts when writing on the performance of a major company. In this way, the individual investor has access to a wider range of opinion on a company than would otherwise be the case.

There are a number of grey areas, which shouldn't be overlooked, but which are often part of public relations activity. For example, exhibitions or trade fairs, and the provision of promotional items, occasionally fall under the public relations function's remit, but should ideally belong to marketing or a specific promotional department. This is also true of some of the items mentioned above, such as sponsorship. Sponsorship might be image building for a major group, but it might also be an element in a marketing strategy, designed to raise product or brand awareness among members of a target audience or niche market. Rather than get into a battle with the marketing people, it is as well to recognise and understand these differences, and agree an allocation of responsibilities which is workable for the organization.

In fact, public relations people will find themselves working closely with other professionals, including personnel, on employee communications, and finance or a secretary's department on investor relations, for example, as well as frequently having a close liaison with marketing. Media relations will often be the service which many of these other groups will be expecting. Personnel might be confronted by a militant union, or be anxious to publicize a new training or equal opportunities initiative, for example, as well as having a keen professional interest in internal communications, such as periodicals and video for employees.

PUBLIC RELATIONS TECHNIQUES

Over the years, a number of techniques have come to be used by the public relations practitioner so that he or she can achieve the various promotional, corporate and employee communications objectives required by employers or, in the case of consultants, their clients. Many of these are well known, although, as we will see when they are examined in closer detail, frequently misused or abused.

The main techniques include:

1. Press or media releases – sometimes also called a 'news release', these are the usual means of communicating news,

whether it be an appointment, a contract, new premises, investment, products, or news about the performance of the organization, usually using specially designed paper.

2. Case histories or studies – these give the audience information on how a satisfied customer was helped by a product or service, and attempt to get the audience to identify with the customer and appreciate the relevance of the product to their own situation.

3. Feature articles – these are usually written from a professional or industry standpoint, in which case they can heighten the image of the organization and its management, but they can, especially in trade publications, be written from a more commercial viewpoint.

4. Advertorials – in return for advertising, some newspapers and magazines will offer a compensatory amount of editorial space, for an article or a case history.

5. Editorial interviews – meetings between the organization and journalists who are either writing on the industry or on the organization itself, and are looking for background information and informed, relevant comment.

6. Event press support – providing journalists attending an event with information on the organization and/or the event.

7. Analysts briefing – an essential element in financial communications, is the briefing of investment analysts or the fund managers of institutional investors on the progress of the business.

8. Financial reports – a prime requirement for publicly quoted companies, this is a technique which can be used to advantage by many other organizations, including quasi-governmental organizations or charities.

9. Political lobbying – ensuring that politicians at local and national, or even supra-national level in the case of the European Community, are aware of the problems and objectives of your organization.

10. Newsletters and publications – these are most frequently aimed at employees, but can also be intended for customers, and range from simple newsletters through to newspapers and magazines.

11. Video and film – more up-to-date than printed matter and with additional impact, always provided that the subject is suited to the medium, and the extra cost can be justified.

12. Conferences and seminars – these are suitable for either internal or external audiences, and can be an effective means of achieving specific objectives, especially when instant feedback is required.

13. Product launches – essential in business, but of course the 'product' could also be a charitable appeal or a major campaign.

14. Special events – these can be sponsored events, or the opening of new premises, visits by customers or politicians, anniversaries, mergers or acquisitions.

15. Promotional items – anything from a cheap plastic pen through to prestige gifts, these can be part of PR, especially on the fraught question of what to give, when to do it, and to whom?

16. Corporate image – the way in which the organization is perceived by internal and external audiences.

Many of these will also impinge on media relations, especially items 1 to 6, 13 and 14. It is fair to suggest that almost regardless of the type of organization, these are the common thread in PR activity. Naturally, a new product for a manufacturer has to be replaced in a charity by a new appeal for funds, or in a government department by a major new policy initiative, for example. Inevitably, as one considers the problems of more effective targeting of media relations, one has to take into account the differences between organizations and ensure that the work of the PR, or media relations, function is aligned with the requirements of one's employer or client.

THE PUBLIC RELATIONS BUSINESS

While it might be tempting to consider public relations simply in terms of the particular task in hand, one also needs to be aware of the structure of the public relations business, and in particular of the relationship between those people who are employed by organizations on their own permanent payroll – the 'in-house' PR functions – and those who provide external advice – the PR consultants. The distinction between the role of PR consultancies and advertising agencies is also worth considering in this context, as are the other services provided for the profession by outside bodies, and the way in which the profession is structured.

PR consultancies

The terminology of 'PR consultancies' and 'advertising agencies' first needs to be explained. While at first it might seem as if these are simply somewhat elevated titles, there is some logic behind them.

Advertising companies are known as 'agencies' for valid historical reasons, in that originally they received commission from the media for the advertising which they placed, and indeed this is still an important part of agency remuneration today, although, as we will see, whether or not it is the primary source of income will depend on the nature of the account. Officially, only recognized agencies are entitled to this commission.

PR consultancies, on the other hand, are supposed to be retained, allowing their clients to consult, as part of their fee structure. The fee should take into account the number of man days per month allocated to the client, on top of which will be the expenses of handling the work, additional time spent on special projects, and a surcharge on work subcontracted to other professionals, including, for example, photographers. Retainers are usually payable in advance quarterly, although sometimes a monthly payment will be agreed instead. Needless to say, this arrangement does not preclude special arrangements with consultancies on an ad hoc basis.

In the public relations profession, it is not unknown for strong passions to be aroused over the question of whether PR activity is best handled by a consultancy or by an in-house person or team, or indeed on the best hybrid solution in those instances when the issue is less clear cut. In practice, the energy involved in such a debate, and the manner in which points are scored off one side or the other, would be better used in assessing the relative merits of either arrangement, or of a suitable compromise, with regard to the particular circumstances of the organization or a particular project or campaign.

Clearly, there are circumstances in which it is uneconomic to appoint a permanent full-time PR person, either on the grounds of cost or because they would be under-occupied. Although one solution to this particular problem would be to have an individual handling PR in addition to other duties, the question can arise as to whether the individual will have the necessary combination of skills and the time, not least because of the demanding nature of the deadlines imposed on certain aspects of PR activity. Much will depend on the individual and the nature of the business, as well as on the number of PR tasks which he or she will be expected to perform.

On the other hand, widely fluctuating pressures can also argue in favour of employing a consultancy, since they will be able to draw upon additional manpower from their own resources when one client, usually referred to as an 'account', is exceptionally busy. The other members of the consultancy team drafted in will have some knowledge of other clients if the consultancy has been well run and has good internal communications and briefing procedures, but even more important, they will already be experienced professionals.

Pressure does not simply consist of issuing a press release or answering the telephone when a major story has been issued. There is a great deal of routine attached to efficient and effective PR, including ensuring that press contact lists are kept well up-to-date, as journalists change jobs or are promoted. Again, ensuring that releases are tailored to the needs of specific publications can be time-consuming, but worthwhile in terms of ensuring that effort is targeted and effective.

Consultancy is not cheap, and should not be if it is done well. There is, if anything, a tendency for many consultancies to keep their retainer too low, and to devote too much time to finding ways of increasing the income to be derived from a particular account. To have the use of a good PR consultant for one day per week will cost as much as a good in-house person could expect to be paid for the whole week. Nevertheless, it is more complex than this, since the consultancy fee will include many overheads not taken into account with the in-house person, whose total costs will be far higher than salary alone would indicate.

PR consultancies might be regarded as having advantages in the following situations:

1. If PR effort is too little or too spasmodic to justify the expense of a full-time in-house specialist.

2. When there are likely to be severe peaks and troughs in the

workload, either due to major product launches, seasonal factors, or exhibitions and events. The typical situation would be one in which two or three people might be needed at certain times, but not at all for the rest of the year.

3. While an in-house person can be justified, there might be the need for a relief in his or her absence, and at certain periods of peak workload.

4. The experience of the in-house person, or even the entire in-house team, is concentrated on a particular aspect of public relations (marketing, or other promotional activity, for example), and the consultancy can provide professional advice in other areas, such as financial or corporate relations.

5. The organization has moved into a new activity or is expanding into a new geographical area, and needs good media contacts immediately. If distance or language, let alone both of these factors, can be added to the equation, the argument in favour of consultancy is reinforced.

6. The organization is highly political and in-house advice is associated with one warring faction or another, and so becomes compromised, in which case the objectivity of the consultant can be vital.

Hybrid solutions

Instances 3, 4 and 5 above support a hybrid solution, in which in-house and consultancy PR people are both employed and work together, providing that the division in work and responsibility is clearly defined. The senior in-house person should also have the responsibility for co-ordinating the available resources, and ensuring that the consultancy is always adequately briefed and its work monitored. In addition, one might have to accept that, human nature being what it is, there are managements who will give more attention to costly advice from an outsider than to that available for the salary of the in-house practitioner. There are even instances in which the appointment of a particular consultancy is related to the lack of self-confidence of certain members of the management team or, on the other hand, to a form of corporate vanity.

It is not unusual for companies largely preoccupied with marketing or promotional support to leave their relations with the financial community to a specialized consultancy. One can also find organizations which have a strong in-house team looking after publications and internal communications, while using one consultancy for marketing and another for financial PR. In other cases, consultancies might be asked to provide support functions, such as press release distribution, although one can commission such specialized services direct. There are also arrangements in which the in-house person is relatively junior, but is guided by an external consultant. Yet another arrangement is for the consultancy to provide one of their own employees to work inside the client's organization as an 'implant'.

It is clear from this that individual needs must provide the guidelines for management considering the most suitable method for handling their public relations activity. Even so, one has to suggest that some of the hybrid arrangements mentioned can have drawbacks. The high cost of using a consultancy simply for press release distribution has already been indicated, while one has to question the way in which a senior external consultant can really guide the in-house person who is closer to the problems and the management, and who must have the credibility to be taken into their confidence so that problems and opportunities can be identified.

On a more positive note, balancing skills by allocating certain tasks to a consultancy while keeping others in-house can be a sensible and practical arrangement. It can also be a sound decision to appoint a consultancy on a short-term contract or on an ad hoc basis to cope with a period of pressure, although one has to be careful, since there is the possibility that the consultancy itself will have to resort to the use of freelance people to supplement its own resources at such times, and this arrangement can only work if tight control is applied and the freelance people have been carefully selected, ideally for their own specialized knowledge.

One should not overlook the fact that many PR consultancies will provide a variety of skills and services in-house, including editing, photographic direction, video production, and design services, which can be a useful resource for a client or an in-house PR team to utilize as and when needed. It can be cheaper to employ such skills direct, either on a freelance basis or in-house, but often there is not the time to find such people when they are needed, and often such skills cannot be justified within an organization.

Merits of the in-house team

So, what are the merits of using an in-house person or an in-house team? There are several to balance out those of a consultancy, and the main ones would be:

1. In-house people are less expensive, even when competitive remuneration is given.

2. Frequent daily contact with the management team means that in-house people are far more likely to discover potential PR opportunities for the organization, especially on the media relations aspects of their work, but also on employee communications.

3. A growing familiarity with the organization and its activities means that briefing can be less formal than with consultancy.

4. In-house people generally have greater credibility with those outside the organization, including customers and the media, because they are identified with it and with the management team.

5. As an extension of 3 and 4 above, the in-house people will often be viewed by the media as being able to offer background to industry problems, creating a further opportunity for building on the relationship between the PR practitioners and the media which is so important to success. Any PR person who reaches this position will find that it is a supreme accolade.

6. In the best managed organizations, PR is involved in senior management decision-making, and this is easier if the individuals concerned are part of the senior management team.

It is important to stress that using in-house facilities should not be viewed purely on cost grounds or should not be used so that briefing can be skimped, or simply because one wants to have a PR person to hand rather than have to arrange a meeting with a consultancy – PR people, whether in-house or in consultancy, should always make themselves available in an emergency, but like everyone else, they also try to plan their day! Briefing will still be necessary, and indeed one might find that overall more time is devoted to PR once an in-house person arrives, as more opportunities for PR are identified, or as PR becomes more closely involved in decision-making. This is inevitable since, after all, the real point is that the significance of the overall image and communications issues is being recognized.

One shouldn't underestimate the informal contact with senior management and directors available to in-house people, since often people will forget about communications problems unless prompted by a chance encounter with a PR person. The significance of an odd remark in the lift, or a few words at the coffee machine, shouldn't be underestimated.

Compromise is often important, nevertheless. In some diversified organizations, subsidiary companies will resist using a central PR function. Every excuse will be used, from cost, if this is passed on to them, to quality of service, if costs are met centrally. Leaving the subsidiaries to make their own arrangements, subject to over-riding central quality control, and if necessary employing consultants, can be one means of keeping all concerned contented. Oddly enough, consultants in such a position are often more aware of the need to keep the parent company PR function in the picture than in-house divisional PR people would ever be.

On a less positive note, many consultants are sometimes pre-occupied with seeking new business, and preparing to obtain this – a process known as 'pitching'. This is one weakness of using consultants, and it has its in-house parallel in a member of staff spending all their time job hunting. Some new and ambitious consultancies spend their days working for their clients, and the nights and weekends attempting to get additional clients, leaving staff jaded and unresponsive in handling the existing business. The best managed consultancies will employ a new business team, leaving the rest of their staff to service the business allocated to them. It is also true that consultancy is a balancing act, with the business and the numbers employed having to be in balance to ensure profitability, so staff numbers are usually kept fairly tight.

ADVERTISING

We saw earlier the difference between PR and advertising, but there are occasions when public relations and advertising will mix. We will look later at the two main occasions when this occurs; the first being 'advertorials', in which advertising is supported by the offer of editorial space, and the second the advertising of an organization's financial performance, which is usually handled by the PR function rather than by the marketing activity, for reasons which will become clear later.

Advertising is frequently regarded as being the most glamourous of activities, and to some extent the image is justified, although it is exaggerated by the lifestyle of some of the more publicity-conscious senior figures in the industry, and by the sycophantic journalists of the specialized press.

Although it is tempting for PR people to take the view that advertising is easier than PR since, after all, having paid for the space or the air time one has relatively strong control over the message, this is an over-simplification. Advertising depends on its acceptability to the audience, which means that a combination of creative skills will be required, while the planning of the advertising campaign, the selection of the media to be used and the frequency of advertisements, require a scientific approach and a substantial level of knowledge and skill. The problems of those in advertising and those employed in PR might be different, and so are the skills, but the problems do exist and the need for professionalism applies to both functions.

Advertising agencies

Most advertisers of any size use agencies, and some will use several, not least because different agencies have their strengths and weaknesses, as do PR consultancies. An advertising agency well suited to consumer advertising, for package holidays or consumer durables, for example, would not be suitable for recruitment advertising or financial and corporate advertising, and vice versa. There are occasions when an advertiser will use different agencies, perhaps taking one agency for business-to-business advertising and another for consumer business, or simply because of a desire not to place too much dependence on a single agency or to be able to enjoy a variety of talent. On the other hand, there are those organizations which prefer to concentrate their advertising on a single agency, even to the extent of dealing with an agency with an international spread of offices and creative teams, especially if the product is one which can be sold in this way rather than adjusted for specific markets. This approach allows tighter control of the overall advertising theme or the message.

Advertising agencies can be changed for a variety of reasons, including the most obvious one, which is that of dissatisfaction with performance or a change in emphasis. The high level of creative input can also mean that the movement of a creative team, or a leading member of a creative team, can lead to a review of advertising and even to accounts following certain individuals from agency to agency. Of course, advertising accounts have also moved because the client involved has been concerned at the number of staff changes within the agency and the lack of continuity.

As mentioned earlier in this chapter, agencies are paid for partly out of commission allowed by the media to recognized agencies. This commission is usually 10 per cent, but might occasionally be as much as 15 per cent. After taking the commission into account, it is usual for the advertising agency to add a management fee of 17.65 per cent to the net cost of the advertisement, and this is the charge paid by the client. This means that for every £100 of advertising, assuming commission of 10 per cent, the cost to the client is £105.85. Since the commission element or the surcharge is a management fee, the client will also be charged for the cost of preparing an advertisement. Increasingly, major clients prefer to pay the net cost of the advertising space or air time, and then pay the agency a negotiated fee on top of this. Apart from major clients, this arrangement is often appropriate if advertising in the media is relatively small, and perhaps most of the costs are those relating to other services such as brochure production.

Advertising agencies compare themselves on the basis of media space or time bought, known as the 'above the line' spend, and then on other items such as brochure or point of sale work which will be regarded as 'below the line'.

Advertising staff

The costs of an advertising agency are high because of the variety of people involved. These include:

- Account staff – will liaise with the client and generally manage the account, acting as a coordinating point.

- Media planners – prepare proposals for a campaign, and will also work with the media buyers, negotiate prices, including special discounts which take into account the volume of advertising placed with a single publication or group of publications, and negotiate for selected positions for an advertisement.

- Art or creative departments – will handle illustrations, as part of an overall creative team, which will also include copywriters.

In each case, the most senior person will be a director, but there will be a substantial number of senior people below this level. There is a tendency for account directors to be non-board directors.

Work such as television commercial production will often be subcontracted to a specialist, but most work on newspaper and poster advertising will be handled by the agency team, unless, of course, the agency confines itself to creative work or is a media planning and buying agency, as opposed to a 'full service' agency. There are also specialist direct mail agencies.

Few organizations handle advertising in-house, largely, one suspects, because the culture of business enterprises or other organizations, such as charities and government departments, conflicts with that of creative people, but one also has to accept that it would be hard to justify or know how to manage such people well within a different environment. Even if the workload is enough to justify this, creative people enjoy the stimulus of working with other creative people. A few organizations have set up their own advertising agencies, but usually these have broken free in the end and established an independent existence. On the client side, the marketing team will handle the relationship with the advertising agency. This is in complete contrast to public relations, which is both a management tool and often a management function as well.

3
The Media

This book takes the premise that media relations is one of the most important aspects of public relations, and as mentioned earlier, that media relations is the conduit through which many other audiences can be addressed and influenced. Media relations is only of limited value in the PR sense if one simply sees it as an end in itself. It should not be viewed in this way. The media, or as some would still have it, the press, do not exist for their own purposes, but to satisfy the interest of their own audiences. One can draw a comparison with investment analysts, whose research is not an academic exercise, but leads to recommendations on which investors will be taking decisions. The media are, however, usually more impartial than the investment analysts since the latter will often be concerned with the longer-term marketing aspirations of the stockbroker who employs them. The journalists working for the media will equally be concerned about the fortunes of their employing newspaper, magazine, radio or television station, but those interests are usually best served by a reputation for impartial and accurate reporting.

The media and those working in them act as opinion-formers. This does not mean, as mentioned already, simply influencing opinion on matters of public policy or politics, but on other matters as well. Such matters as which product is the best, and which company offers the best service, or which has the better long-term prospects for investors, and even which charity comes closest to meeting its own exacting standards, are all matters of interest and concern to the media, and to those who are influenced by their reporting and by their comments.

Accusations of inaccuracy or bias in the media often result from two major problems. Inaccuracy often arises because journalists cannot get the information they require quickly enough, and are working against extremely tight and inflexible deadlines which mean that they require instant responses, or as near to instant responses as can be provided. Secondly, some inaccuracy is confused with a lack of attention to detail, which is a different problem altogether. Space constraints in publications or the limitations on air time in broadcasting, as well as the the limited time available for researching and writing a story, will impose limitations on the amount of detail which can be included in a news report.

This is difficult enough with a quality newspaper, but more difficult still with a popular newspaper, and even more difficult in broadcasting. If the quality newspaper can give a story 1200 to 1500 words, in a middle market tabloid that will be reduced to 600 words or so, perhaps less, and in a popular tabloid 100 to 200 words. Broadcasters have to convey much of the news with no more than two or three sentences per story or news item. This might seem to be unfair to you, but fairness is the preserve of the reader, listener or viewer, whose attention span is limited. Remember, there is a difference between producing a learned paper on a significant scientific development for an interested scientific audience, and in conveying information on a new product, a policy, an issue, an appeal, to an audience which is not involved and which often has other matters on its mind. Targeting means tailoring the message to the audience, as well as selecting the appropriate media to reach that audience.

As for bias, there is sometimes bias of a political nature, and occasionally a newspaper or an individual journalist will be riding a pet hobby horse, attempting to convey his or her political or moral feelings, or a private concern, for example, for the environment. Nevertheless, most journalists when given the facts in straightforward lay terms, when treated with openness, honesty, courtesy and with due understanding of the pressures on them, will be looking to provide a balanced account. If one is dealing with a new product, the best journalists will, of course, be comparing it to others on the market, so the point is to emphasize those aspects which make it different, and if it is simply another 'me too' product, accept that this will reduce your chances of media coverage. The first, or different, products are more likely to be newsworthy than those which are simply copies under a different brand name, even if the brand has a better reputation than its rivals. Journalists do appreciate that if one financial institution offers a savings account, so will others, but they are working for the reader, not for the financial institution, and are expected to convey information which is accurate and helpful.

As indicated earlier, there will be occasions, for which media relations will not be the best or the most precise PR technique. It will be for the individual practitioner to make this decision and advise the client or the employer accordingly, but generally media work will be of the utmost importance, even if only a part of the role.

We have seen earlier that it is also argued that media relations is too imprecise an instrument, but this really is a criticism of the way in which this aspect of PR is handled.The media themselves will always welcome any attempt to target material more carefully, since they are the fiercest critics of what might best be described as the 'scattergun' approach favoured by far too many PR practitioners.

We will look at media relations in greater detail in due course, but for the moment, the objective is simply to understand the variety of the media, and the way in which it functions. The role of the media in the UK is especially relevant, and indeed its diversity in the UK is far greater than almost anywhere else, not least because of the presence of both a strong national media and good regional and local media as well.

National differences in the media must not be forgotten, however. Increasingly, PR practitioners will be expected to look outside and beyond their own national boundaries, and be able to adapt to the different circumstances of an overseas market, for example. This is not to suggest that they should be looking for employment abroad, but instead a reflection of the demands of their UK-based clients or employers. Even today, such longer range cross-border PR activity is difficult to handle, because of differences in the media and in language, so this can give rise to circumstances in which support from a locally-based PR person or from a good consultancy based in the target market can be invaluable.

To take just one such example, the UK has a strong national press, but not every country has this. Spain and the United States, for example, have daily newspapers with a stronger regional bias, and a less substantial national daily media. Against this, countries with a weak or limited national daily press will have strong weekly news magazines, of a kind which do not really exist in the UK, and which in recent years have defied attempts at their creation, such as the short-lived *Now* magazine. In spite of their excellence, British publications such as the *The Economist*, cannot be regarded as being in this category, and neither can the Sunday newspaper colour supplements.

It is an important element in successful media relations that the differences between the local free newspaper and the national press is fully understood, as are the needs of the specialized trade and technical press, and of broadcasting, and that national differences are also appreciated, both within the UK itself, and, of course, in the wider, truly international, context.

THE GENERAL PRESS

In using the term 'general press', one is referring to any newspaper or periodical which is not specialized and does not aim at a specific audience. In effect, it means the national and regional daily and Sunday newspapers, and weekly local newspapers. One would exclude weekly or monthly periodicals intended for women, the elderly, or teenagers, for example.

National and regional press

In the United Kingdom, the term 'national press' usually refers to the London daily morning newspapers and to the Sunday newspapers also published in London. Nevertheless, one should also show concern for the sensibilities of the Scots and the Welsh and recognize that the term is often taken to include those daily and Sunday newspapers published in Edinburgh, Glasgow and Cardiff, to distinguish the Scottish and Welsh national newspapers from the 'British'. Viewed in this light, there is no such thing as an 'English' national press, since with the exception of the *Daily Mirror* and *Sunday Mirror*, which have Scottish counterparts in the *Daily Record* and *Sunday Mail*, all of the London morning newspapers circulate in Scotland, Wales and Northern Ireland. Such distinctions might appear to be pedantic, but since the object of the exercise is to improve media relations, it is worth remembering that attitudes change away from London.

By contrast, the term 'regional press' refers to the morning newspapers published in many English cities, and in Dundee and Aberdeen as well, while the Belfast newspapers generally tend to be regarded in this light, by the Irish as much as by their mainland counterparts. There are also a few regional Sunday newspapers, such as the *Sunday Independent* in Plymouth and the *Sunday Sun* in Newcastle. The evening newspapers published in many British cities are not generally regarded as being regional, although few would suggest that they are quite as local as some weekly publications. On the other hand, Sunday newspapers will be either national or regional.

In contrast to genuinely local newspapers, which are published weekly or, in a few instances, twice weekly, the daily and Sunday newspapers published outside London are at pains to ensure that their news and features coverage includes a substantial proportion of national and international material, as well as financial and other news, in addition to regional news or placing national developments into a regional context. For example, if there were to be changes in the Defence Budget, a newspaper in the West Country would look at the impact on the region's military bases, army regiments and on defence-based manufacturing industry. Stock market fluctuations might also be reported generally, but with at least a mention of the impact on companies based in the region or with a strong presence in the region. At one time, the *Western Daily Press*, published in Bristol, advertised itself on television as being 'Your international, national and local newspaper'.

The common characteristic of all of these newspapers is that the news which they carry is intended to be as fresh as possible. A major feature following the news of a few days earlier and explaining the background, might be useful, and certainly is intended to be so to the reader, but it is most definitely not 'news', and one must never forget that this is their prime purpose. Sometimes news of a specialized variety will appear in a specific edition, on a particular day of the week, when there might be a personal finance or a motoring column, but this is to distinguish between information of a more specialized and less urgent variety and that of general immediate interest.

Newspaper operation

A typical national newspaper will have a full staff of journalists who will be divided between reporters, usually working on the news desk or the sports desk, photographers, controlled by the pictures editor or the pictures desk, and specialized correspondents. There will usually be a features department, handling background articles and sometimes specialized pages or sections, such as those dealing with travel, women, gardening or other specific topics. Apart from the sports pages, the financial or business pages will form another regular section, while there might be weekly sections on personal finance or other subjects. In the UK, the term 'city' refers to business and financial news, while in the United States, it generally means the general news desk, reflecting the more localized, and sometimes more parochial, coverage of many American daily newspapers. Specific journalists might be designated as a correspondent or editor with responsibility for a specialized subject, although on regional newspapers and evening newspapers, one journalist might have several such roles. The difference in staffing between the national and the regional newspapers reflects the smaller scale of the latter's operations. A London-based national newspaper such as the *Daily Telegraph* has a circulation each day in excess of a million, while even the *Financial Times* has a circulation of more than 250,000, with the popular tabloids often having circulation figures of 2 million or more. The *Scotsman* has less than 100,000 daily, with the *Herald* (until recently the *Glasgow Herald*) doing rather better than this at well over the 100,000 mark, while the *Western Daily Press* has just over 100,000. Obviously, smaller circulations mean lower revenue, and therefore less money to spend on a full range of specialized correspondents. Some of the shortfall in news and features content is compensated for by news agency material, or syndicated features, and, let us not forget, good quality material generated by public relations people!

On these publications, the cross-over between advertising and editorial is limited to specific special advertising features. Perhaps the one exception to this rule has been the relatively recent introduction of 'paid for' appointments columns in the *Herald* and the *Scotsman*.

London newspapers accept appointments free, although most are extremely selective about the posts mentioned, usually only covering the most senior appointments in the main companies, although until recently the *Financial Times* was somewhat more relaxed on this matter with a substantial daily list of appointments. The idea of charging for such items seems to have started in Dublin. Since most companies do not believe in paying for appointments to be published, charging has generally resulted in a significant reduction in the calibre of appointments featured, while the newspapers concerned still find that they have to run the most significant appointments free of charge because of their news value.

The gaps in the newspaper's own sources of information and its specialized correspondents will usually be filled by a combination of freelance journalists and 'stringers', the latter being freelancers but with a more regular relationship with the newspaper, and the news agencies. Some freelance journalists will syndicate a column to several newspapers, usually evening newspapers. In addition, newspapers will receive material from the main news or press agencies, including the Press Association, which was founded by British newspapers to provide news, Reuters, which handles international news, and foreign agencies, as well as many regional agencies throughout the British Isles, who will look for an angle to a story which arises in their area which will enable them to sell it to a newspaper either in London or in another part of the country. As an example, if someone from Scotland is involved in an accident in Wales, a local news agency will ensure that the story is reported and despatched by wire, facsimile machine, telephone or in some cases a computerised link, to the main Scottish newspapers and broadcasting stations.

It is usual for regional newspapers to have a London office, sometimes sharing an office and its staff between several titles within the same group. This is in contrast to the main editorial offices in the regions, where morning and evening newspapers will share the same premises, but have separate editorial teams and news desks. The main exception to this policy of separate editorial teams is in Liverpool, where one editorial team works on both the morning and the evening newspapers. To the casual observer, the existence of separate editorial teams for a morning and evening newspaper published in the same town or city and by the same proprietor might appear to be an example of double manning, but there are good reasons for this, apart from the need to keep working hours to a healthy maximum! The style of many morning and evening newspapers will be substantially different, and as mentioned already, the approach of the morning newspaper will be towards regional news, while the evening newspaper will tend to be more localized in its approach. The ability of the London office to share staff reflects its role in handling national and international news for its head office in the regions, and a considerable concentration on business and financial news as well. A further reason for maintaining separate editorial teams is to emphasize the different character of morning and evening journalism so that as many people as possible buy both newspapers!

Sunday newspapers also maintain separate editorial teams regardless of where they are published. Sunday newspaper journalism is different from that of the dailies with more attention paid to features material and especially those which put the events of the preceding week into context.

Attempts in the UK to produce a single, combined morning and evening newspaper, the so-called '24 hour newspaper' with customers expected to buy two or more editions each day, have been markedly unsuccessful. 'Seven day' newspapers which minimize the difference between the daily and Sunday newspaper, and use the same editorial team, have also yet to prove themselves.

The local press

Local newspapers are usually weekly, although can be twice weekly or even fortnightly. They can be divided into the traditional 'paid for' publications and for the newer 'freesheets'. It is not unusual for a regional newspaper group to have its own series of weekly titles. Editorial staffs are much smaller on weekly newspapers than on daily newspapers, and local newspapers are often the first step on the career ladder for many journalists destined to go much further in journalism. Even so, it is worth noting that the editorial staffs on the freesheets will be even smaller than on the paid for newspapers, and the publishers of many paid for newspapers will also publish a freesheet as well, usually as a defensive measure against the appearance of a freesheet from a rival company. To make the maximum use of the available journalistic and other resources, many local newspapers will be part of a series with substantially the same editorial team and a substantial degree of common content even though there may be half-a-dozen or more titles on the newsagents' counters, each serving a particular town or village. One problem for PR practitioners of this type of approach is that a news item or article intended for one town can appear in half a dozen, and sometimes prove to be misleading.

Finance

The financing of newspapers is such that a quality national newspaper, such as the *Daily Telegraph*, probably only has a quarter of its costs accounted for by the cover price, with the remainder paid for by the advertising, while the popular national newspapers, such as the *Daily Mirror*, will have half their costs covered by the cover price. Most newspapers and magazines which are paid for will try to have 45-55 per cent of their space devoted to editorial, but on free newspapers, this figure can be less than 10 per cent, although the best do much better than this. Weekly newspapers are more likely to grant editorial space to accompany advertising, and this is especially noticeable in the case of the freesheets, the worst of which show a marked bias towards the advertiser.

Deadlines

Deadlines vary, but for evening newspapers can be very early in the morning of the day of publication, while for morning newspapers, the deadline can be as early as late afternoon on the day before publication. The best morning newspapers will work past midnight on stories in London, and after 10 pm in the main provincial centres, and a few can still produce a final edition at 4 am, but this is reserved for major news, dealing with war, accidents, disasters and political developments, while company news, short of a major bankruptcy with massive redundancies, will not be handled. Problems over distribution mean that early editions of morning newspapers need to be available shortly after 9 pm of the day before publication.

Weekly local newspapers normally have a deadline of Wednesday for Friday publication, and to be sure of publication in a particular week, one should think in terms of Monday for Thursday publication and Tuesday for Friday publication.

Sunday newspapers will often close their special news and features pages relatively early in the week, and it will only be the hard general news which is handled on Saturday. The news likely to be handled up to, and sometimes past, deadlines will usually be of accidents or major upheavals of one kind or another – product news, when it is of interest to the press, will need to be issued with deadlines kept in mind.

TRADE AND PROFESSIONAL PUBLICATIONS

The wide variety of occupations and business activities in the UK is mirrored in an equally wide and varied trade and professional press. The quality of such publications varies perhaps even more so than in the case of the general media, while again there are publications which are free, those which are paid for, and those available on controlled circulation to registered readers, as well as those issued to members of trade associations or professional bodies. Publication can be daily, as in the case of *Lloyds List*, the shipping and insurance newspaper, or the *Morning Advertiser* (the newspaper for publicans), but these are the exceptions, and most publications in this category will be weekly or monthly, and in some cases, especially for the more learned journals, publication might be quarterly. Not all of these publications will be interested in product news, or indeed appointments, and so a good knowledge of the publications covering a particular market is necessary, unless one wants to issue material which will simply irritate editors.

The best trade publications, such as *The Grocer* and *Flight International*, have high standards, and will keep to tight weekly deadlines to provide hard news for their readers, but others take a more relaxed attitude, and many will show little urgency over publication of product stories, so that the duration of special offers to retailers, for example, might have expired by the time the news appears in print. A further blurring of the distinction between editorial and advertising comes with publications, including some covering office equipment, which will offer to use colour material, providing that the separation costs are met by the company on whose behalf the story has been issued.

Some trade publications provide reader enquiry cards both for advertising and for editorial, which can be of assistance in analysing the suitability of publications for certain product stories, and comparing the effectiveness of advertising and media relations. Using this system, one manufacturer of office planning charts found that its PR achieved four times the number of enquiries as its advertising.

One problem is that many businessmen are more concerned about editorial mentions in their trade press, seen only by their competitors, than about coverage in periodicals and newspapers read by prospective customers. Peer group recognition is a powerful force in assessing the effectiveness of a media relations campaign.

Deadlines for the trade and professional publications will vary widely, but on weekly publications appearing on a Friday, one should always think in terms of a Tuesday or Wednesday deadline, at the latest.

It is a relatively easy matter to discover which publications will be interested in product stories, which will accept appointments stories, and which will be interested in background features or case studies, or the others which will only take academic papers. A quick look at a sample of any publication will give strong clues to its interest and that of its readers, but a quick flick through the pages of *PR Planner* will also show exactly what any publication will be, and will not be, interested in. There are other clues. Publications published by, or for, professional institutions or academic bodies will seldom want product news, and those professional publications accepting appointment stories will only be concerned with those which deal with their members. If a publication appears quarterly, it is likely to have an academic bias, and not require news at all. Weeklies, by contrast, are likely to be heavily orientated towards news, with a lower level of features content than, for example, a monthly publication.

Neither truly general nor truly trade and professional are the many regional and other business publications. These are also often free, but sometimes paid for, and are usually monthly. There is a tendency for many of them to favour local business, almost to the extent of seldom being outspoken, but others do attempt to produce a worthwhile periodical of genuine interest to the readers and worthy of the attention of advertisers and those handling media relations.

SPECIAL INTEREST PUBLICATIONS

The variety of business and professional publications has its parallel in a whole range of publications aimed at people with special interests, or who belong to readily identifiable groups, and in many ways these are similar to the trade and professional media, except that relatively few of these are free to the readers. Many of these publications are strongly consumer orientated, and so while news about new products or services will often receive editorial mentions, the publications will be far more careful in their analysis of the new products than some of the weaker trade publications would dare to be. This is no bad thing, especially if the product really is worthwhile.

These publications are of importance, especially when media material is being targeted to reach a particular audience. It would be wrong to confine details of a worthwhile product to such publications since there will often be a substantial additional readership for the more popular topics in the specialized columns of the general press. True, few general newspapers will review pop music, but they will have theatre, film and book reviews, and reviews of major concerts, ballet or opera productions. The general press will not review a new light aeroplane, but they will handle new motor cars. New computers, even for the home, have still to receive more than token attention in the general media, but new implements for the garden or the kitchen can often receive their due coverage.

The less 'newsy' specialized publications include many intended for young people and for women. The features-orientation of such publications entails heavy planning and so material is often collated several months in advance of publication, in contrast to the daily newspaper which is mainly preoccupied with the previous day's news. In the case of trade and professional publications and specialized consumer interest or hobby magazines, a good idea of their forthcoming features, with deadlines, can be obtained through subscribing to a regular service, *Advance*, which also includes much on forthcoming editorial plans for the more general press and regional publications as well.

BROADCASTING

The British Broadcasting Corporation (BBC) provides national, regional and local radio in Britain as well as an outstanding world service, funded by the Foreign Office, which broadcasts in a large number of foreign languages. The BBC provides national television, with a number of regional programmes.

The independent broadcasting stations are far more fragmented, with local independent radio and regional television provided by a large number of franchise holders. There are 14 regional independent television stations, although HTV, covering the West of England and Wales, provides different programming for these two areas, and in London, the weekend and weekday broadcasts are divided between two companies. Independent breakfast television, now provided by GMTV, is the only national independent, and is restricted to broadcasting in the mornings. A new nationwide independent is planned for the future, and this is currently referred to as 'Channel 5' while the outcome of the franchise award is awaited. While the independent television companies receive their news coverage from Independent Television News, a separate organization, the local radio stations receive their news from Independent Radio News, operated by LBC, one of the London radio stations. There is interchange between BBC radio and television news services nationally and regionally, but seldom does this occur in the independent sector. Individual radio and television contractors will provide news for their respective national services. The emphasis is different, and on such matters as programming the BBC operates nationally, but makes exceptions for regional programmes: despite improving coordination, the independent television companies still operate in a way exactly opposite to this – something worth remembering when looking at the broadcast possibilities for a sponsored event, for example.

It is important to remember that individual independent broadcasting stations will have different programmes and varied attitudes to local or regional news. Coverage can be improved by concentrating on good regional or local news angles rather than wasting time attempting national coverage which might prove elusive. In some cases, a good regional story might be referred to the ITN or IRN news desk if it is felt to have obvious national implications, but one should never count on this.

Sponsored programming as such has only recently been permitted in the UK. Otherwise, radio and television programmers have to make a clear distinction between advertising and the rest of their output, and the volume of advertising permitted in any one hour of broadcasting is also limited. These distinctions are not adhered to with such rigidity overseas. While the BBC does not transmit advertising, many foreign state-owned broadcasting stations supplement their revenue from advertising, with notable examples occurring in the Irish Republic and New Zealand.

Obtaining coverage

Obtaining coverage on the broadcast media is more difficult than in the press for the simple reason that the amount of news which can be transmitted is limited by time considerations. Nevertheless, carefully targeted items of regional or local interest can succeed in a limited area, while the screen-based news and information services, such as Ceefax on BBC 1 and BBC 2, and Teletext on the two Independent Television channels, also contain vast quantities of information daily. Broadcasters can seldom offer editorial coverage in return for advertising, and this is especially so nationally, but there can be opportunities on local radio for providing services, such as stock market reviews, which raise the profile of the organisation. Recent changes allowing sponsorship of programmes in the UK have been accompanied by restrictions which are intended to ensure the editorial impartiality of the programme-makers. Sponsors of programmes must not be directly involved with the subject of the programme, and so this means, for example, that Barclaycard can sponsor a holiday programme, but would be prevented from sponsoring a programme on personal finance. The benefit to Barclaycard of such a sponsorship is clear, since many people will pay for holidays, and for expenses incurred whilst on holiday, using a credit card.

One new development which can help companies and other organizations reach a large audience is the availability on BBC 2 television of off-peak night time broadcasts which can be video recorded by those interested in watching them. Programmes must be factual and not promotional, and the activity is handled through a production company, BMH, and not by the BBC itself.

The wide range of specialized features programmes dealing with topics as diverse as motoring, gardening and cooking can also provide opportunities for product promotion, but television can demonstrate the weaknesses of a product even more graphically than a review in a newspaper, so beware!

4

Matching the Media and the Organization

The diversity of media in the United Kingdom might appear daunting at first, but once the organization and its aims are understood, and media can be selected to match the organization's media relations requirements, the whole process becomes manageable. The diversity then becomes an aid to careful and precise targeting of messages attuned to the interests of specific audiences.

First of all, it is important that the management of any organization which the PR practitioner has as an employer or a client appreciates the role of the media and the opportunities which the media can provide. This book is not for those whose interest in media relations does not extend beyond the reactive, but unless managements appreciate the importance of responding to the media and making use of the media, proactive PR becomes pointless. No journalist will tolerate, still less respect, an organization which is willing to use the media, but which promptly puts up the barriers when a situation becomes difficult.

It is important that media enquiries, and most especially those which arise from criticism or a crisis affecting the organization, are handled efficiently and politely. The term 'no comment' in effect acts as confirmation, and at best leaves only one side of the argument presented. Good managements see the opportunity to advance their case as more than a counter to criticism, but instead as an opportunity to convey a positive message about their organization and the progress which it is making.

The media work to deadlines which differ from those of normal office hours, and there is no organization which can afford to have its spokesmen unavailable outside normal office hours, at weekends or over a public holiday. It matters not at all that the business might appear to be low key and inoffensive. Factories and retail premises can burn down or be subjected to criminal action. Accidents do happen and mistakes are made in even the best managed and most successful organizations. Charities and pressure groups can make mistakes and receive criticism just as much as any business concern.

Secondly, before matching the media and the organization, it is also important to ensure that the public relations practitioner is not himself or herself a mismatch to his employers and their business. There is a belief in some quarters to the effect that public relations or media relations skills are completely portable or transferable, and that anyone who can handle public relations for a pharmaceuticals manufacturer, for example, can handle PR for a fashion house or a transport operator. One can seldom divorce PR activity of any kind, but especially external or media relations skills, from the product. There can be a certain degree of movement between industries or sectors for the PR professional, but one has to accept specialities and also the need for at least a degree of empathy amongst those concerned. If one has strong moral or political objections to the profit motive or to private enterprise, commerce and finance might not be suitable, to put it mildly. If engineering or pharmaceuticals leave one confused by the technicalities, these are obviously the wrong sectors. Someone who has scant regard for his or her appearance, with little dress sense or a feel for colour might not do well with a fashion house. Putting a more positive and constructive light on this aspect of PR, someone who enjoys the dynamism of transport and doesn't mind trouble shooting or crisis management, would find work for an airline or some other transport operator fulfilling.

FOUR STEPS TOWARDS MATCHING THE MEDIA

Matching the available media to the organization might appear a difficult task, but it is one which requires logic, a methodical and slightly analytical approach, diligence and a little creative management. There should be little sense of mystery in this duty. The process can be reduced to four simple steps:

1. What is the organization's function?

2. Who are the audiences essential to its success?

3. What message or messages does it need to convey?

4. Which are the available media to reach the target audiences?

Function

Organizations and their level of visibility vary enormously. Primary industries such as minerals extraction tend to have a relatively low public profile, and are often unknown to the consumer or the specifier of industrial goods because they are at opposite ends of a chain which will include intermediate industries, such as forging or component production, manufacturing, and distribution. In transport, for example, few will have heard of the operators of gas carriers or bulk chemical tankers, but many will be aware of the main ferry or cruise ship operators. This tendency towards a low profile is not necessarily a bad thing. Primary industry does not usually need to sell to millions of consumers, but may instead have a small number of large customers buying its raw materials for processing. In addition to such customers, it will be anxious to maintain contact with potential and existing investors and their advisors, and with the communities in whose area it engages in its business and recruits many of its workers. Indeed, the cynics might suggest that primary industry only attracts a high profile when there is a major accident or incident, often resulting in loss of life or damage to the environment.

By contrast, the manufacturer of consumer goods will be dealing with millions, or even tens or hundreds of millions, of customers and potential customers. While some companies sell direct to the consumer, it is still more usual for sales to be through distributors and retailers, providing another substantial and fragmented audience who will not only wish to learn about developments themselves, but will also hope that sufficient consumer interest is aroused to bring enquiries into their premises. The situation with companies selling to small businesses is not dissimilar; again there will be a substantial number of potential customers, and often a network of distributors as well.

This need to understand the nature of the sector is not confined to business, but also affects the operations of charities, pressure groups, political parties, trade unions, professional bodies, academic institutions, and so on. The need for effective media relations is endless.

The audience

Understanding the organization or the sector in which it operates is paralleled by a need to understand the audiences. Consumers differ as an audience from those responsible for the management of a major business, for example. In some sectors, the customer, in the sense of the user, is not the specifier of the product. This is apparent in many sectors. The office worker using a word processor computer terminal could be regarded as the customer, but in fact he or she is more properly the 'end-user' of the product, their employer being the customer. The specifier, whose attention has to be gained, is a member of the management team who might enjoy substantial delegated authority in purchasing decisions; in other cases the specifier might simply chair a committee. The other obvious example of the way in which the customer can become a blurred concept is in medical treatment, and this can be complicated by the fact that the patient can also make some of the decisions, on the purchase of patent, as opposed to ethical, pharmaceuticals, and the selection of private health care or insurance. The doctor will specify the appropriate ethical pharmaceuticals in most cases, but might be guided by an approved list.

In some cases, the end-user can influence the customer in making decisions. Some road transport operators will follow the preferences of their drivers in specifying vehicles or ferry services, for example.

The customer does not have to buy a product in the conventional sense. The person making a charitable donation is accepting the message about the charity and its work, and making a decision as a consequence. The individual voting for a political party has decided to accept its message and provide his or her support.

Sometimes customers need, and expect guidance. While many people will listen to the salesman before buying a car or a household product, they will usually make their own decisions. In financial services, by contrast, they may be more inclined to follow the advice of a consultant, being guided over the best choice of mortgage or insurance, for example.

It is wrong to assume that all audiences consist of customers. Investors and their advisers, suppliers, distributors or retailers, the local community, politicians, prospective and existing employees and their friends and families, are also there to be influenced.

The message

Accordingly, messages are diverse. Organizations wish to see their product receiving due media attention, but they might also wish to raise their profile in other ways. A financial institution might wish to express an opinion on the state of the economy or the consequence of government policies or some international development, and in so doing, it can raise its profile and should be able to ensure that its opinions will convince the audience of the quality and depth of its management. This is because those concerned have come to appreciate that companies which are asked to provide a comment are recognized by the audience as having a certain authority in their field, and regardless of size, some advantage in quality over their peers.

Once again, this is not the prerogative of business. If a situation arises on which a charity could comment, a higher profile and authority will be gained by the charity which the media decide to select for an opinion. The average reader of newspapers, or listener to a broadcast, will assume that the charity concerned has something to say, and that those running it are regarded by the media as being the true authority on the subject.

This enhancement of the image is also closely allied to ensuring a situation of mutual benefit with the media. Every organization has messages which it wishes to convey, but the media are not there simply to carry these messages as free editorial. There has to be a degree of newsworthiness and interest amongst the audience before editors will commit space to a product story or a charitable appeal and, after all, advertising space is available for those who must communicate at all costs. Journalists trying to put an economic or political development into context, perhaps examining its impact on business or the general public, always appreciate those organizations who are willing to help them with a comment or opinion, or even to examine the likely outcome on an economic model and provide the result. One can also move a step beyond this, and publish the results of research into a matter of current interest. Research need not always be serious to attract media attention, but it should have some impact and general interest. The Halifax Building Society survey of children's pocket money each year gains many column inches in the press, and a considerable amount of air time on the major broadcasting stations, because it is a perennial subject of public interest and curiosity. Another building society attracted much attention and comment when it published its research into mortgage arrears, and this was not least because the research dispelled some widely-held misconceptions, and also showed the society in question in a favourable light.

In a consumer-led society, the findings of the Consumers' Association are always of interest to the media, and while there is no doubt that these provide a service to the public, one of the Association's primary objectives in announcing its findings to the media is to attract additional members to the Association. This is not being unduly cynical, and it is also worth recognizing that another objective is to ensure that the media coverage provides additional force for any criticisms or recommendations made in the reports. Much the same can be said about the Automobile Association and Royal Automobile Club findings on such matters as the efficiency of garages in servicing cars, for example. Charities which conduct research and then publish the findings have similar motives and objectives, attracting additional support for their cause, either in funding, voluntary assistance, or in the sense of a change in official policy which will benefit their aims.

The enhancement of the image amongst the target audience is doubtless important in all of these cases, but the reminder to journalists, that all-important intermediary audience, is also vital, so that they realize that organization X will have something worth saying and does not simply issue press releases on uninteresting run-of-the-mill products, or minor appointments.

Available media

The final step is to understand the media available, and what interests them. In the previous chapter, we saw how a story which might not be of interest nationally could be highly newsworthy regionally or locally, and indeed could also be of value in trade or business publications. The ability of organizations to generate such interest varies. It is easier for manufacturers, for example, than for retailers. Why is this? The reason is that free editorial coverage goes first and foremost to those who are different. If a manufacturer launches an electric car that will differ in some way from anything produced by its competitors, but in hundreds of dealers throughout the country the same product will be available. The same goes for most consumer goods. The only way in which a retailer can hope to obtain coverage in the media without paying for it is to have a genuinely exclusive product; it sometimes happens, and companies which, for example, import wines which are not available through any of their competitors' outlets will stand a chance of being mentioned by the wine writers, but only if they handle the media relations well and the product is both distinctive and of the desired value and quality. Always remember that the wine writers or any other specialized correspondents, are endorsing your product or service and their own credibility with readers and with their peers will be at stake!

Obviously goods which are produced to the specification of the retailer have added interest and are more likely to be covered in the food, wines, fashion or other similar pages of the consumer press. Clearly this still won't be enough to ensure that a supermarket chain's own brand of baked beans will be noticed by the media, since that would be regarded simply as another 'me too' product to sit alongside one or two major brands on the shelves. Nevertheless, something which is sufficiently different and distinctive, and genuinely new, may attract attention.

The best examples of this in media relations for retail business come, of course, not so much from the purveyors of food and clothing, but from the financial services industry. New products from banks or building societies can usually expect some mention. Once again, the impact will depend on a number of factors which, apart from those already mentioned above, must also include the ability of the organization concerned to reach a substantial market. If for example, a mail order financial product, such as those marketed by the erstwhile Guardian Building Society, is interesting, it can expect coverage, and so too can a product sold over the counter at the local branch of the Halifax Building Society. Generally, for a national newspaper, a product available only through the branches of a small building society whose network was confined, say, to a single county, would not hold sufficient interest or benefit for the majority of its readers and would be unlikely to be covered. It is, however, possible for the product to receive national press coverage if it is of such quality that a slightly different slant can be taken; the product being presented as an example to others of what can be done.

It would be foolish to ignore the fact that most national daily and Sunday newspapers devote more space to personal finance products than they do to almost any other consumer product. One only has to look at the motoring, gardening, home improvements, cooking, food or wine pages, or even the arts and books sections in comparison. On the other hand, there are a whole range of periodicals which cover the home and garden aspects of life as well, most, despite sexual equality, angled primarily at a female audience!

One has to recognize that some products are simply more likely to attract general media interest than others. It is still easier to attract attention for a new model of car than for a new word processor or home computer, for example, and while both of these products will gain specialized media interest, only the car is likely to be covered in the general press. Despite the interest of a number of enthusiasts, word processors and home computers attract as little general media interest as other household consumer items. Fashion, and new food products, or wines, are also interesting to the general media, and so too are holidays and travel as well as gardening. The media shouldn't be criticized for this: they know what will and what won't work, both from experience and the need to satisfy *their* customers.

In the next chapter we will look at the difference between news and features, and the role of visual images in media relations.

MATCHING THE MEDIA AND THE ORGANIZATION

So, which media will be likely to take an interest in your organization? Much will depend on the product and the market or audience, but there are a number of general guidelines which one can adopt, and which will help, especially if one is new to the organization and attempting to make early improvements to the cost-effectiveness of its media relations.

For those with responsibility for an organization's media relations, the diversity of the media must be welcomed, because it is through this diversity that effective targeting becomes possible. At the same time, in the UK the presence of a strong, nationwide, general press, and the existence of the broadcasting networks, also mean that messages attuned to a general audience can obtain a suitable airing. This all contributes to the flexibility which the PR practitioner enjoys. It also means that even if an organization's management has lost its objectivity, and has come to believe that their achievements deserve front page treatment in the national newspapers, they need not be completely disappointed because they will receive the coverage which they deserve, perhaps on an inside page or in a special section, in a regional or local newspaper, or in their industry's specialized media. The fact is that few stories truly warrant front page treatment; there is only so much space on a page! For a British national newspaper, and for many regional papers as well, the front page exists for international and national news; truly the life and death material which causes the newspaper-buying public to stop at a newsagent. This is another aspect of the media which cannot be over-stressed. Journalists, whether they be reporters, editors, or whatever, exist to serve the reader. The reader does not buy a publication for its advertising content, yet without the reader advertising would be pointless.

Far too many stories which warrant good coverage from specialized publications or even in particular sections of the general press such as motoring or finance are lost to the world because someone, somewhere, has made the mistake of over-rating their value to the general reader. If one is lucky, the news editor, if time permits, might leave the story in the in-tray of a specialist colleague, but all too often the pressure is such that anything which misses the mark goes into the waste bin, or, to use newspaper terminology, the story is *spiked*.

So what really does interest the media? Before we move on to consider the difference between news and features, or even the value of a good photograph, we need to consider just how organizations differ, and how they need to have a clear appreciation of the likely media interest in their activities. As a rule, newspapers are most likely to be interested in news or features material which means something to the majority of their readers. Something is newsworthy because it is new and because it is different.

Getting the media interested

Earlier we discussed the difficulty which retailers have in promoting themselves when the products they are offering are not unique. There are a few ways around this. In the case of the motor vehicle mentioned, a dealer might obtain coverage in the motoring column of the local newspaper by offering the motoring correspondent the loan of a demonstration vehicle for a few days, or even a week. The condition being that the journalist would mention that the car had been loaned by the dealer. The essential prerequisites for this technique to succeed are:

- The local newspaper has a motoring column. They won't start one just for you.

- The column is handled locally, and not syndicated by an agency or a journalist attached to a group of newspapers and based some distance away. Apart from anything else, the larger catchment area could mean that most of the readers will be closer to a rival dealer selling the same product.

- The car has recently been launched and has not been covered by the newspaper in question, or any of its rivals.

- Another dealer in the same area hasn't done this already.

- That the editor or the motoring correspondent can undertake that there will be a free editorial feature, without an advertisement having to be taken, in return for the loan of the car.

If one is selling motor cars in, say, Guildford, it is sufficient that the readers of the *Surrey Advertiser* and the *Guildford Times* know about the car, and a wider audience doesn't matter. Many of those reading these newspapers will also have read about the car in the national newspapers, perhaps they will have seen it on BBC2s 'Top Gear' programme, and a few, but a relatively small number, will have read about it in the motoring magazines. The role of the local newspaper coverage is to inform the paper's audience that the car is available locally from a particular dealer. It isn't newsworthy, but it can make a good feature, although first the dealer has to treat the motoring correspondent seriously and provide a sufficently long loan of the test car for it to be properly evaluated. If any of the other reviews of the car have been less than enthusiastic, the opinion of the local journalist might be helpful, although, of course, he or she might agree with the national press. While journalists generally try to be objective in reviewing cars, plays or whatever, they have their own opinions and preferences, and one has to accept this.

Nature of the organization

It is essential to understand the nature of the organization. For a start, is its business such that it can be categorized as local, regional, national, or international? Next, what does it do? Is it part of a primary industry, such as minerals extraction, agriculture or fisheries; intermediate industry such as iron and steel production, or manufacturing, and if the latter, is it manufacturing components or completed goods, or perhaps engaged in processing, such as dairy products? The service sector has grown over the years, and so the business might be in distribution, including the retail trades, transport or travel, professional services, such as the legal profession, accountancy, surveying, advertising or public relations, hotels, catering or leisure, or financial services. An important and diverse sector is property and construction, which also has a retail element in estate agency and surveying. Yet another important sector is publishing, whether it be books, newspapers or magazines, and, of course, one shouldn't forget broadcasting. There are many activities which are not always regarded as being businesses at all, especially by those working in them, such as the performing arts, the visual arts, trade associations, professional bodies, academic institutions, hospitals, museums and zoological or botanical gardens. Then there are pressure groups, trade unions, charities, local and central government, or even international organizations, such as the European Commission, the North Atlantic Treaty Organisation, and the International Monetary Fund, and, of course, political parties.

These differences have a marked impact on the way in which media relations have to be handled. Primary industry does not have the same media interest as many other sectors, and when it does arouse interest, the story is more likely to be industrial or environmental than promotional. Component manufacturers have a profile within the industries which they serve, and their media involvement is most likely to be industrial or with the specialized trade media. Manufacturers of finished products are of greater interest to the consumer media, as are others who might not regard themselves as manufacturers, such as publishers, because consumers, and the media which they receive, are 'product conscious'. Retailers usually interest the media when they have a genuinely exclusive product to sell.

It is fair to consider the performing arts as a product, because after all, one hopes that consumers will pay for tickets. Professional bodies and trade associations are more likely to be concerned with the media from the industrial or political angle, and even when a qualification is being promoted as a product, it will not be of interest to the media as a whole, but to management and careers writers. On the other hand, the work of a charity or the campaigns of a pressure group, could be of considerable media interest if it has popular appeal or arouses widespread concern.

Many organizations fit into two or more of these sectors or categories. For example, the AA and the RAC are pressure groups lobbying on behalf of motorists, but they also provide a service for motorists, assisting them when their vehicles break down, and for organizers of events, providing temporary direction signs. In addition, they are retailers or distributors, offering maps and other items of interest to motorists, publishers of handbooks and guides, and the AA has also become a travel agent.

Some organizations show substantial vertical integration. The best example in terms of a high consumer and business profile must be the oil companies, which explore for oil, develop oil fields and extract oil, transport the crude oil, refine it, distribute petrol and other oil products, and market and sell it, often through their own retail outlets. The gas and electricity companies have a similar role, but also act as distributors and retailers of domestic appliances. There are differences of course between these energy companies. For example, in Scotland, the electricity companies manufacture and distribute electricity, but in England and Wales, the practice is to be either a generator or distributor. Gas and electricity companies sell appliances, whereas the oil companies do not sell motor vehicles.

Other organizations show horizontal integration. P&O, for example, is no longer simply a shipowner, but also a road haulier and a property and construction company as well. Such companies are more along the lines of conglomerates, but even before this there are instances of horizontal integration such as, for example, the office products manufacturer ACCO, which also produces office furniture, planning charts and visual aids, rather than just simple filing and paper clips.

We will look at the way in which media relations should be organized for such companies in Chapter 11.

Suitable media

Next it is important that one considers the media suitable for an organization. Should it be general or specialized, and if the former, is it local, regional, national or international? The latter can be divided into the media suitable for people with special interests, in the case of the consumer media, or the trade and professional media of interest primarily to the business-to-business markets.

Finally, all the foregoing will be largely determined by various audiences. Consumer or business, for example? Can the audience be differentiated by age or sex, nationality, religion, ethnic group, or by their social standing, or simply by whether or not they are married or single, parents, pet owners, or whatever? Business people can also be sub-divided many times over, by profession or their level in an organization as well as by the sector in which they are working. The audiences might also be opinion-formers, such as politicians, journalists or investment analysts.

Because most media relations programmes will be aimed at a

number of audiences, and because most organizations fall into more than one sector or category, and the messages will also vary, a good deal of planning and thought has to go into a media relations programme. Let's take a few examples to illustrate this.

Examples

Let's take first the case of the office products manufacturer, Twinlock, now part of the American-owned ACCO Corporation. The company operated through several brands: Twinlock, producing office furniture and filing products, and Sasco, producing wall planners and presentation aids, both operated through distributors; while another two brands, Carson Office Furniture and Shannon Datastor (sic), with the latter offering filing and storage products, sold direct to customers.

The prime objective for Twinlock's media relations was to obtain coverage in two trade magazines, *Stationery Trade News* and *Stationery Trade Gazette*, both of which were aimed at the wholesale and retail business. Until an in-house PR manager was appointed, no thought was given to reaching publications aimed at the decision-maker or purchaser of office products. The problems were compounded by an earlier decision to drop all but the largest retailers and reach the smaller retailers through wholesalers, whose salesmen, of course, had no particular brief for the products of each manufacturer.

To resolve this failure of media relations, attention was paid to raising the company's profile with a number of specialist publications:

- The computer media were targeted, so that the company's growing range of computer products could be supported by a mixture of product stories and background articles, some of which used research findings.

- For traditional products, other user-media were selected. Press releases, case studies and photo-caption stories would be angled at a particular trade or profession.

- Regional business magazines were provided with articles on office and computer management, supporting local dealers.

- A newsletter was introduced for retailers, so that they became more conscious of the company's products and were able to specify these from their wholesalers. Since people like to read about others like themselves, the newsletter also included case studies of dealers enjoying a success with a particular product or products.

The newsletter was in fact a re-introduction, since the company's founder had launched a newsletter so that he could maintain contact with his customers, the retailers, when his sales force was called up for active service during World War I. More importantly, the opinion and background pieces which senior management had ghosted for them in trade publications produced far more interest and enquiries than the simple product stories which littered the pages of so many office and computer publications.

A further step was to provide 'think' pieces offering opinions on the industry or advice for the users or specifiers of office and computer equipment. These generated rather greater levels of sales enquiries than the product stories which continued to be provided.

The same approach was taken for Twinlock's subsidiary, Sasco, although here the emphasis on different customer groups was increased, while there was less opportunity for 'think' pieces, other than in the media aimed at retailers.

A different set of problems arose with the Bristol & West Building Society, whose name, in particular the '& West', emphasized a local connection, which did little to promote its role as a quasi-national society. While the specialized property and personal finance writers of the main national newspapers knew the organization well enough to appreciate its broad spread of branches, there was a need to raise the profile of individual branches in their own catchment areas. The techniques was simple: matching branch catchment areas with newspaper circulation areas, press releases were 'localized', with the branch managers' names substituted for those of the Chief Executive or other senior personnel. Newspapers were sent these releases from the Press Office so that a relationship could be developed with the specialized correspondents on regional and local newspapers. The local manager's name on a release provided the local angle, while the mention of the manager or the branch in the story when published reminded readers that the society had a branch in their town. The next stage was to offer articles on home ownership and other related topics, all of which were prepared centrally, but which appeared once again as if written by the local manager. A further stage in this evolutionary process came when local managers were encouraged to accept invitations to appear on local radio, often handling 'phone-in' programmes.

Research by the Society's economists was also published, raising its profile and adding credibility to media relations which became more a mutual benefit to the Society and the media, rather than simply a selection of 'PR puffs'. On a simpler basis, research on property prices by branch managers in Scotland led to a regular feature in the *Dundee Courier*, again supporting the branches.

A few detailed points also aided this success. The regional managers for Scotland and for Wales had their titles changed for media use to 'Manager, Scotland' and 'Manager, Wales', recognizing national sensibilities and the fact that these countries have their regions just as England does.

Advertorial

While advertorial as such lacks the credibility of free editorial, there are occasions when a specific need can be attained by using advertorial. If one opens a new branch in a small town or village, often that will be newsworthy enough for the local newspaper, but in a larger town, with more news, one new retail outlet is meaningless in news terms. In such instances, advertorial in weekly newspapers can be a useful means of bridging the gap, and ensuring that the event does appear in the appropriate media. Good quality and well balanced advertorial, written and presented in a professional manner, can work. The mistakes to avoid are those of over-hyping the product or the organization, and of making the editorial content too long; always attempt to write to the same length as the newspaper in question would use for genuine editorial matter.

A new slant in advertorial has arisen through the decision by the BBC to offer 'paid-for' television programmes which are broadcast on BBC2 during the night. Obviously, even with shift workers, there are few people watching television at such hours, but the system is based on the assumption that interested audiences will use their video recorders to tape programmes which they can watch later. It also assumes that the organizations concerned can reach enough of their target audience to make them fully aware of the programme being broadcast.

As mentioned in the previous chapter, the programmes are arranged in conjunction with a production company, BMH Productions.

One early use of the service was a broadcast of coverage of the annual general meeting of Scottish Power, an electricity generating and distribution company privatized during the early 1990s. Companies wishing to broadcast the proceedings at their annual general meeting can let their shareholders know of the timing by including this information when they mail their annual report. In the case of newly-privatized companies such as Scottish Power, such broadcasts overcome the problems of reaching a large and fragmented shareholding and also overcome the difficulty which many employee shareholders would encounter if they wished to attend the AGM.

Costs are fairly high, at around £40,000 for a typical 30 minute programme, plus production costs. Obviously, an event such as a meeting would require three or four cameras, professional directors and producers, and would cost far more than a relatively simple company video programme for employees of the kind with which most large and medium-sized companies would be familiar.

In none of these examples was any existing media relations activity abandoned.

5

News, Features and Photography

Although it might be unfair to suggest that media relations is primarily about news coverage, since features activity also looms large in the work programmes of many practitioners, nevertheless, news coverage is all-important for many employers or clients. It is vital that practitioners are aware of the difference between news and features, the way in which they can complement one another, and the importance of photography in adding interest to the newspaper or periodical coverage.

News and features material can occasionally be artificially stimulated, as we will see in the next chapter, but the best and most worthwhile exercises will have substance, without which media relations activity is likely to be hollow and insubstantial. Too many weak stories, too much manufactured news and features material, too many poor and irrelevant photographs, and the patience of the journalists will be exhausted. It is essential that no PR operation, whether it be in-house or by consultancy, ever does anything which undermines its credibility and integrity. Once lost, such qualities are difficult, if not impossible, to regain.

One should never say that something is news when it isn't. Nor should one ever put oneself into a position where the news is so weak that it fails the test of media questioning.

INTO THE NEWS

News value

Human nature being what it is, it is not unusual for the news value of a new product or service, or perhaps a development such as a new branch or a factory, to be greatly exaggerated by those whose proximity to the story is such that they lose their news sense. This is an understandable reaction, especially for those who have laboured long and hard, and remained close to a project or campaign, and it is one reason why the PR practitioner must remain as objective as possible. It also explains to a great extent why so many PR people are drawn from the ranks of journalism. News value can be hard to quantify, and it can be difficult for anyone who has not had newspaper experience to develop that most important PR asset, the true 'nose' for news. They also need the strength of character to be able to withstand pressure to over-claim, or overrate the news value, which sometimes comes from those closely associated with a new development, and even, sometimes, from the marketing professionals who one would hope to have some objectivity of their own.

In spite of this, it would be wrong to assume that this difficulty in appreciating the true news value of a story always emerges as an exaggerated impression of the story's worth. The opposite can, and does, happen, with the value of a story being underestimated. There are many good stories which are not appreciated fully by those involved. Sometimes this is simple modesty, or perhaps a fear of having someone pick fault with a speech, for example. Usually, it is a case of specialists underestimating the impact of a particular project or development, or failing to understand the interest of the outside world. Unfortunately, there are also occasions when, having been awakened to the news value of a development, the specialists overlook the general reader, and the general newspaper journalist, and drown the story in technicalities as the press release is drafted.

News value varies, and it can be hard to quantify, still less explain, to the uninitiated. That instinctive or intuitive judgement which can appreciate the impact of a story, and decide which publications or broadcasting stations will be interested is something which requires hard work and sensitivity as well as intelligence and an ability to understand the role of the media and their interests. It is important to understand that something which is useless for the national press, for example, could have considerable local or regional impact. A manufacturer might simply need good trade and technical press coverage for a new product to be judged a success. There is even more to it than this, however, since there are other questions which good news sense will answer, such as whether or not there should be a photograph (and what kind of photograph), whether a press release will be sufficient, or whether a press conference or briefing is more appropriate, or alternatively should the press receive a sample or a demonstration?

Maintaining objectivity

There are many factors to take into account. For a start, the superlatives, so beloved of advertising and marketing people, are taboo to serious journalists. Genuine 'firsts' or 'bests' are rare, as is a truly 'unique capability'. News value requires advantages to be stressed, but without the use of superlatives. Unfortunately, there are those in marketing who believe that if they fool the PR person, they will also be able to fool the journalists, forgetting that many journalists have a very good idea of what is right, and what isn't. Good specialist journalists will often know more about the market – what is new or merely a 'me too' product, and even what is likely to appear next – than the marketing specialists, or their PR advisers.

The *Financial Times* once described a much-hyped Japanese sports car as being for those who knew little about sports cars since its suspension and handling were dated, as were many other features. The real impact of this damning but well-deserved criticism was that it would be noticed by those who wanted a sports car, knew little about them, but wished people to believe that they knew what they are buying. The true enthusiasts will have made such judgements already – the journalist is expected by his readers to tell them what is good, and what isn't. If such a journalist describes a car as particularly good, then that praise is also highly regarded and beneficial. This illustrates again why PR, and especially media relations, is so important.

Of course, news doesn't have to be commercial or product related. New charity campaigns, reports by pressure groups, the results of research, all of these have a news value. Sometimes news value is reduced because, after all, such material simply states either the obvious or what one would expect a particular, subjective source to say, but well constructed arguments, of significance and targeted to the appropriate media, can, and do, receive coverage.

Specialist stories

One simply has to look at the work of specialized journalists in the general media to realize that they handle the merest tip of the vast amount of news which can be found in many specialist publications. This is not to suggest that a specialist story might not have something for the general public. Leaving aside the public's interest in such matters as travel or finance, for example, sometimes there is an 'angle' of interest to the man in the street. Sometimes this can be achieved through the use of a good photograph, for example, but on other occasions there might be something in the story, such as the implications for employment or the environment, which will provide the necessary element of general interest. Profits, or losses, will be of interest, and so will major orders or new contracts. The *Financial Times* contracts column will take news of contracts of less than £1 million in value, but a local newspaper close to the factory handling such a contract will give the story considerable prominence, and so too will the trade press. Indeed, even much smaller contracts would attract localized media coverage. One word of caution, however, is that, again, much depends on the media, and their own perceptions of their audience. What would appear to be a good story for a newspaper in a small town, might well be overlooked by the London *Evening Standard* or the *Manchester Evening News*. A contract worth £500,000 or so might well be covered in a trade paper dealing with commercial vehicles, but it would be regarded as insignificant for *Flight International* simply because even an order for a single small airliner would have a value well in excess of £10 million.

Some news has a compelling urgency. For example, when building societies or banks change their mortgage rates, everyone wants to know, and the story will appear in the next morning's newspapers. A move by a single building society or bank will be news if it is the first to do so, but of course, it is much less newsworthy if a bank or building society is tenth in the queue to announce a change to its mortgage rate. On the other hand, change the investment rate, and it may have to wait until the next personal finance feature is published. The reason for this is quite simple – mortgages are essential and affect disposable income, while investment products are optional.

Press releases

The main means of getting news to the media is through a media release or, as it is still more usually known, press release. The basic rules for drafting a press release are:

1. It must be brief, with no unnecessary words or pointless

phrases such as 'announces' or 'is pleased to announce'. Never state the obvious, and remember that superlatives are taboo for professional journalists.

2. Leave adequate space at the top for the newspaper sub-editor to write instructions to the printer and to add his own headline – two inches should be sufficient. Leave a one-and-a-half inch margin on the left hand side of every page for editorial amendments and any additional instructions. For the same reasons, never type with single spacing, but use one-and-a-half or, if possible, double spacing. This also makes the release easier to be read in a hurry.

3. Put the date at the top – so that the news editor knows that the story is still current.

4. Look for a short, factual, eye-catching headline. The duty news editor will be 'sniffing' 50 or 60 stories a minute, and may be short of newspaper space or broadcasting time, so one has to work hard to ensure that your story is the one which will catch the attention.

5. The main facts of the story should be included in the first paragraph, for exactly the same reasons in 4 above, but also because if space is short or if the newspaper is just about to go to press, this can be used on its own, and give the reader all he or she needs to know.

6. Ideally, any quotes should be attributed to a director or other senior executive to be worthwhile, unless the story is intended for the local media, in which case the local manager will be the right person, or for the specialized media, in which case the most senior specialist could be the correct choice. The term 'a spokesman said...' really belongs to the press after an enquiry, and should never be used in any statement issued to the media.

7. Keep each paragraph tight, with no more than three sentences, and, in the case of the first paragraph, just one or two. It has to be easily read and understood, just as most newspaper paragraphs are also kept very short, even in the quality newspapers. If a substantial volume of background or technical information is necessary, either prepare a separate press release for the technical media or, alternatively, add a supporting background document.

8. Press releases are not sales documents, and do not need to have every detail contained within them. Newspapers seldom need that quantity of information nor do magazines, even if they are aimed at a trade readership. Broadcasters, especially on news programmes, attempt to make every word count; on radio and television, many news items are covered in just a few sentences.

9. Remember that a press release is not a legal document, and so while it shouldn't be defamatory or misleading, it is not necessary to sacrifice style to legal correctness, and very few press releases should need to be cleared through the organization's legal advisers.

10. A brief concluding statement about the nature of your business, or other activities, can be helpful if the organization is not too well known.

11. End the release with the name and telephone number of a contact, with an out-of-office-hours number as well, since many journalists work outside normal office hours. This should be typed on after the end of the release – itself clearly marked by 'ENDS', to avoid confusion – and never printed as part of the press release paper, just in case the individuals concerned move on to another job, or are simply absent on leave.

12. If the subject of the story is worth a good photograph, make sure that one is provided, with a concise and useable caption attached to the back. If a brochure or price list, or a sample of the product is likely to be useful, this should also be added.

13. If a sample of the product is likely to be useful and it is a practical proposition to provide this, then do so, but often it can be a good idea to offer samples in the contact number footnote since those sent through the post and left lying around newspaper offices can, and do, get lost.

14. If the journalist is likely to require time to research and write the story, allow extra time for this, if necessary using an embargo to reduce the chance of the story breaking too early, if only in an incomplete and misleading form.

FEATURES

Features have two purposes, one is to inform, by providing

additional background to the news or to bring the reader up-to-date on a development of interest, the other is to entertain. Sometimes, a feature can do both – the regular travel and motoring reviews are good examples. On certain subjects, or developments, features can expand on the news, explaining the relevance and the implications of a new development, while there are other regular features which suppliers of various products will find useful in helping to keep their products in the public eye. An example of the way in which features can sometimes work is that a major new venture or new product by a company might be covered on the news pages, but the features pages may well carry background on the reasons for the new development, looking at the implications of the company's strategy, or for the plans of its competitors.

The relevance of the regular specialized features to those working in public relations is straightforward and sometimes even slightly mundane, but important. It is difficult to make news out of a well-established product, although there are exceptions, such as major new orders or milestone stories which demonstrate the success of a product, in terms of so many passengers carried, cars sold, children rescued, etc, since this is not the preserve of those marketing goods and services, but can be used by charities, government, and others. There is an opportunity, nevertheless, to maintain audience awareness of the product by attempting to ensure that it receives coverage on the features pages. Holiday destinations, personal finance products, household or garden products, all of these can be mentioned in regular reviews, just so long as the journalists concerned are kept up-to-date on the price and availability of the product. Features of this kind are usually reviews of what is available, and update the readers on recent developments, such as a new high interest savings account or a new ferry service to a holiday destination.

Naturally, many of these features will contain information which provides an indication of the way in which the product has worked. New cars will receive attention when first introduced, but some journalists will review their experience of a particular model, usually one which has been allocated to them or to a colleague by their employers, after a period of time has passed (a year is often the ideal) or a certain mileage reached. Journalists can be invited to revisit a holiday destination. If they haven't first hand experience of their own, journalists might look for satisfied or dissatisfied customers, or conduct a comparison between, for instance, cars with a similar specification, or children's savings accounts, or the estimates provided by different double-glazing contractors, to suggest just a few examples. There are those whose products benefit by comparison, and they are not necessarily the newest, the cheapest, nor the most expensive products.

In-house features

There are opportunities for features prepared by PR departments or consultancies to be offered to newspapers. The most obvious example of this is advertorial, where space is provided for editorial contributed by a company in return for the purchase of a certain amount of advertising space. Once confined to local newspapers, this has spread to regional newspapers and to some national newspapers, usually in the guise of special supplements. While this might appear to be an opportunity for PR, the practice is recognized for what it is by the reader, and does nothing for the integrity and credibility of journalists or the newspapers which employ them.

PR people handling certain types of work will be fortunate enough to be able to provide feature articles which do not need to be supported by advertising. Ideally these should not mention specific branded products, leaving the 'by-line' (the name and position of the 'author' of the article) to promote the product or organization. Banks and building societies are well placed for this type of feature, providing newspapers with articles on buying homes or financial services, but this benefit is not unique to them. Many other businesses, such as solicitors, accountants, travel agents or tour operators, and retail chains specializing in home or garden products can all provide sound advice, in this form, and in so doing, enhance their standing, as well as boosting their editorial coverage.

PHOTOGRAPHS

There is an old adage about a picture being worth a thousand words, and while this might appear to have become something of a cliché, there is more than a grain of truth in the concept. We will look more closely at photography in Chapter 8, but it is worth considering the relevance of photographs with press releases and features.

Of course, not every subject lends itself to a photograph. It is difficult to photograph such concepts as mortgages or life assurance, but many products can be photographed, some need to be photographed, and even campaigns by charities or pressure groups can find expression in photographs – starving children, injured animals, the elderly, are in fact extremely good subjects for the photographer.

The role of photo-journalism in the news media has to be understood. Most newspapers and magazines use photographs, and contrary to popular belief, newspapers do not maintain vast armies of photographers. Even a London-based daily newspaper might have fewer than half-a-dozen photographers, and will depend heavily on material provided by news agencies. Sometimes, PR photographs will be used, if the standard is suitably high. There are risks, of course, since a photograph with too obvious a display of the company name or logo might well be cropped, so that this disappears. Picture editors are even more fussy about giving free publicity than their colleagues on the news or features desks: a cynic might suggest that this is because they receive fewer invitations to lunch!

For the PR practitioner, the value of a photograph is that it really does say more than a thousand words, provided that it is the right kind of photograph – and that there is a good, concise caption. It might be that the newspaper or magazine will only use the photograph and caption, which is much better than nothing being used at all, or it could be that the existence of a really outstanding photograph will ensure that more space is devoted to the story as the press release and the photograph appear together. Some journalists will ask for an opportunity to photograph the product rather than use a PR 'hand out' photograph, and this approach should always be encouraged since the story is more likely to be used if newspapers know that they will not all be using the same photograph – editors like to ensure that their approach is different from that of their peers. Of course, this isn't always a case of rejecting the PR photograph – on one occasion, the author supplied the *Daily Mirror* with a photograph of a product, and then, at their request, a sample of the product for their own photographer; in the end, the story appeared with both the newspaper's and the PR photographs!

The use of naked or semi-naked models will make the photograph less, not more likely, to be used. On the other hand, the use of a good professional model, male or female, and dressed appropriately for the product's application, can provide scale and life to a product photograph and lift it above the dreary run of 'still-life' photographs which look as if they have been lifted from a catalogue.

It is a worthwhile exercise to compare the photographs of cars or other products in newspapers with those which appear in the manufacturers' publicity material. There is a difference. Again, look at newspaper photographs of personalities, and compare them with the terrible standard of photography which accompanies appointment or promotion stories. This is probably one of the main uses of photography for PR practitioners, but it is one of the most neglected. Even though the appointments columns seldom contain interesting photographs, there are opportunities for lifting this much neglected area, and of course such photographs are important when accompanying articles ghosted for the individual concerned, or on other occasions when management photographs are needed.

There is also a technical as well as a creative aspect to this question of the type of photograph which newspapers or magazines will want, as we will see in Chapter 8.

Never ever assume that newspaper photographers will turn up, no matter how important the event! Instead, always invite them to major events, but ensure that you have your own photographer available. After all, the Wright brothers' first aeroplane flights were ignored by the press, despite the two brothers' excellent reputation as glider pioneers, but thanks to their own foresight, photographs do exist of that memorable day.

ESTABLISHING RELATIONSHIPS

As mentioned earlier, PR people are specialists in their own profession, and while the best of them will gain a first class appreciation of the industry for which they are working, they are not technical people able to talk in depth about what makes a particular piece of technology work, for example. There is a view in some quarters which suggests that PR people, and those in sales and marketing as well, can easily switch from one organization or industry to another, and be equally effective, but this is to ignore the need for the right aptitude and the necessary empathy. To be frank, and realistic, people cannot switch from working in fashions to working in defence equipment, from working in pharmaceuticals or some other chemical industry, to working in financial services, and there are other deeper, perhaps more personal, problems which have to be appreciated if one is to work in the charities sector, politics or in a pressure group.

There is, of course, room for some considerable specialization. A doctor who becomes a medical journalist, and then works in public relations for the medical profession, a pharmaceutical manufacturer or for a health authority, could be the ultimate specialist and achieve considerable credibility. Such people are a rare breed, however, and there is always a danger that they will become too involved, too close to the subject, to be effective communicators with the general press. There is something to be said for the argument that if the specialists cannot convince their PR people, or get them to put the message into clear and concise English, they should keep quiet.

Understanding the organization

It is vital that new PR people are given a thorough grounding in the workings of the organization and the way in which it fits into the overall scheme of things, its relationships with other organizations or industries and its position compared with that of its competitors. A thorough induction programme is a necessity, and opportunities must always be open for the PR people to familiarize themselves with different parts of the organization, and especially with new subsidiaries or new products. The public relations function must fully understand the business, whether a commercial organization, or some non-commercial activity. More than this, the PR function must also be aware of and able to understand the philosophy of the organization and its strategy for the short, medium and longer term. The difficulties or shortcomings of the organization must be understood, and in particular any difficulties with particular markets, or groups. Anticipated difficulties are obviously another part of this: how can PR people provide sound advice unless they have a thorough appreciation of the situation? In short, it is essential to be as open and trusting with the PR function as one would be with a solicitor or accountant, and for the same reason: the quality of professional advice is dependent upon the full picture being understood. If the PR person cannot be trusted, he or she is in the wrong profession.

PR and decision making

Implicit in such arrangements is the need for the most senior PR person in an organization to be able to deal with the most senior person in any function, and indeed, the senior PR person should only report to the chief executive or chairman, or the equivalent in other bodies. It is not necessary for PR to be represented on the board of directors, but it is necessary for PR to be a part of executive or management committees taking important decisions, so that PR can express an opinion, advise and, of course, influence decisions or the way in which certain decisions are implemented or communicated. Taking a decision without PR advice and then expecting PR simply to communicate that decision is not enough.

Take just one frequent occurrence in a publicly quoted company, the need to make an announcement to the stock exchange, as an example. Stock exchange announcements are important and carefully regulated to ensure that there is equality of information among those who may wish to trade in the shares of a company. Those who have additional information are restricted in their ability to buy and sell shares. Sometimes, companies have little choice over the timing of company announcements, for example, if simultaneous announcements need to be made on stock exchanges in different countries, or when another company involved in a major transaction has decided to make an announcement, but usually, it is possible to exercise a certain amount of discretion. There are occasions when company announcements are in time for analysts and journalists to follow up the announcement, leaving more time for questions to be asked and for greater preparation of an article to get the message across to readers. This also implies that there are other occasions which are less suitable; many investment analysts and financial journalists are suspicious of any company which makes its announcements as the stock markets close on a Friday or on the eve of a public holiday. A responsible PR person, being aware in advance of the likelihood of any announcement, will advise on the best time. No respectable organization relishes its announcements being treated with suspicion, not so much because of what they contain, but because of poor timing.

It is necessary to get the essentials right so that media contact, and indeed contact with other interested groups or audiences, can be handled efficiently. One should never forget that often media enquiries require an immediate response, or as near immediate as possible. It is not unusual for a journalist to telephone within minutes of a deadline for a newspaper to be printed or a radio or television news bulletin being broadcast. It is not just a question of who can speak to the media, and how far they are allowed to go, but also of who vets media releases, and even of who can authorize expenditure on entertaining the press? Visits by the media and by investment analysts or politicians need to be authorized, but who decides whether or not such an event should happen, who should be invited, what they should see, or whom they should meet?

MEETING THE PRESS

The best relationship which can be created with the media is one which is based on mutual trust, and on the efficiency and sensitivity of the PR function. One also has to understand and accept that the interests of the media and of the organization are not necessarily the same. One should never waste the time of journalists, and never forget that they may be working on a number of stories at the same time. It is not unusual for a journalist to have invitations to half-a-dozen or so press conferences or receptions on any one day, with most of these being arranged for late morning or lunch-time. Journalists do not appreciate being invited to a press conference when a telephone call or even a simple press release would do. A press conference is really only suitable for a significant story, when it has the advantage of ensuring that a consistent message is not only given to the media, but that they also have the opportunity of asking questions of directors or senior management. These questions are also handled more consistently and efficiently at a press conference than if a dozen or so journalists were to telephone individually. While journalists do not like sharing questions and answers with their peers, and rivals, they do appreciate that a press conference also means that they learn more than might be possible in a one-to-one interview, and of course, good questions and answers often stimulate other questions.

Nevertheless, never organize a press conference when one simply wants a press reception at which hospitality and the chance to meet the press is more important, and the news value is insignificant. Never organize a reception when there are not likely to be enough senior people present, since the press don't want simply to come along to meet PR people. Never organize a press conference when a telephone call will do, and never telephone when a simple press release will do.

Journalistic jargon

Some of the jargon of journalism has passed into everyday language, but unfortunately it has become garbled and misunderstood in so doing. It is important when speaking to the media, either over the telephone or face-to-face, to remember the correct terminology. Never forget that everything is 'on the record' unless one makes it clear that is not so before speaking. One should also remember the following:

- *Quote:* This really means a comment, so that the journalist can write or report that someone said this.

- *Off the record:* This means simply that it is not to be quoted but is instead for the background information of the journalist. Too much of this will make an interview worthless unless, of course, a journalist has asked for, and been given, a background briefing 'off the record'.

- *Non-attributable:* There are times when one is happy to see something reported, but might be embarrassed at seeing one's name or one's organization mentioned, so a non-attributable comment can be reported and even quoted, but without the source being identified. In newspapers, this might appear as 'a source within the industry', or 'an observer of...', for example.

- *No comment:* This leaves the media to draw their own conclusions, unless one is able to say that one cannot comment for a good reason, because a particular topic is *sub judice*, for example.

- *Embargo:* This restricts publication or broadcast of a news item before a certain time, allowing journalists to prepare and research a complex story. Unnecessary embargoes can irritate or be broken, or in the case of a minor story, ensure that it is consigned to oblivion. One should be sensitive to pressures with an embargo; something embargoed to benefit the Sunday newspapers may be used by the Saturday newspapers. A way around this is to release the story by wire or facsimile transmission in time for journalists to work on it, but without an embargo. The correct terminology for an embargo is to head the press release with:

  EMBARGO: NOT FOR PUBLICATION OR BROAD-CAST BEFORE [time] HOURS, _ DAY _ DATE'

  Obviously, there are dangers, and for example, stock exchange price sensitive information distributed under embargo might enable journalists to profit from news not available to investors generally – another instance of an embargo not always providing an easy answer to a PR problem.

Contrary to popular opinion, the media by and large are not desperate for another free lunch, if they ever were, although the media, in common with the business community, may simply be reflecting the increasing pressure of modern times, when a long and alcoholic lunch or a working day spent on the golf course is an extremely rare event indeed. Those journalists who are always available for lunch or a reception, tend to be the less effective and least helpful to your cause. These are journalists who will drift from one event to another, seeking the one with the best food and drink, rather than obtaining the story and spending time in the office developing the story, seeking comments from others interested in a particular development, and even investigating whether their editor will also require a follow-up feature as well as the news story.

Broadcast interviews

Such phrases as 'off-the-record' obviously don't apply when dealing with a broadcast interview. It is usual in such cases for the interviewer and the interviewee to have a brief discussion before the interview starts, so that the theme of the interview is understood by both. The interviewer will want to be certain that the interview is worthwhile, while the interviewee will need to know the general direction of the questions so that he or she can be certain that they have the facts at their fingertips. If suddenly asked to give an interview over the telephone by a broadcasting station, it is wise to allow yourself, or your employer or client, at least a few minutes to assemble thoughts and facts.

In giving a broadcast interview, do bear in mind:

1. Keep answers short, but not too short. Never say simply 'yes' or 'no', but instead produce a brief sentence of explanation or information. This helps the interviewer and also gives you a better broadcast image to the listener or viewer.

2. For the same reasons always be polite, and unless the situation is grave (as in the case of a major accident), try to smile occasionally.

3. If an otherwise intelligent interviewer asks some questions to which the answer seems to be obvious, be patient. The interviewer is asking questions for the average listener or

viewer and attempting to establish background for the layman.

4. Confine yourself to making one or two points. You might simply appear as a 'sound bite' making a succinct comment, especially on a news programme, or you may have a minute or two. Too many points in a broadcast interview would be lost on your audience, even if you are allocated the broadcast time.

For those likely to be interviewed frequently, media training is essential. This should be handled by specialists, taking at least two and no more than four potential interviewees at a time. Too many on such a course will prevent the individuals receiving the personal attention which is necessary, but on a one-to-one basis, such training becomes too intense. People do need to see others being trained so that they can learn from each other.

While not a substitute for media training, companies such as BBS Productions of Bristol do produce an excellent series of training videos for press, radio and television interviews. These are an ideal introduction and good pre-training material. They will also give an employer or client with little understanding of the role of the media and the way in which they work, a grounding in the subject.

6

Seizing the Opportunities

No organization has an automatic right to coverage by the media. The media exist to serve their audience, who are their customers. Without regular listeners, viewers or readers, no medium could survive and no one would consider that medium as a suitable vehicle for advertising. The loyalty which many have for particular journalists or for their newspapers or periodicals, radio or television programmes, is not easily won, and those concerned with their journalistic reputations ensure that these are jealously guarded.

That being so, good stories will always be of interest, and even more so if the story is well presented by the PR practitioner, is supported by just the right number of important facts, and is sufficiently well targeted to reach those who are likely to be interested. Equally it must not be wasted on those journalists, programme producers or their researchers who would be unlikely to take any interest at all.

To be completely frank, poor targeting is not only likely to damage the organization's reputation as it becomes synonymous in the minds of the media with non-stories, it is uneconomic and inefficient. The waste in postage, courier or facsimile transmission costs, in paper, and in the time taken to prepare, copy, collate and envelope material which the recipient does not want, all adds up to a waste of money, of time and of opportunity, when more productive work could be being done by those involved on a futile exercise.

It should be clear already that news and features material, the very essence of the work of a press office, does not happen, still less appear in the press, by accident. The effective public relations practitioner will be looking for worthwhile material in addition to reacting to requests for the issue of press releases by a number of functions within the organization, including not only marketing, but often the chief executive's or finance director's offices, or, in the case of a charity, the appeals director. Articles might be demanded by newspapers or magazines, especially those who are looking for a contributed piece rather than seeking an interview for one of their own staff writers.

Often, clients or employers will not fully appreciate all the attention to detail and organization which results in good media coverage. A true professional, however, will make such matters appear straightforward to the uninitiated!

MANAGING NEWS AND FEATURES

Often, managing news and features means looking for topical events. This could mean ensuring that products are brought to the attention of the media at suitable times of the year, always providing that the lengthy production periods and tight deadlines are kept in mind. It might mean providing predictions or suggestions before the Chancellor of the Exchequer announces his Budget each year, or responding immediately to the Budget speech. Pressure groups, political movements and even charities might have much to say about the contents of the Queen's Speech or any policy announcement by the government of the day! Large national and international issues provide a 'peg', in newspaper terms, on which a story or comment can be hung, but so too do local stories, or moves by a competitor, or even interest rate changes, employment figures, inflation, the balance of trade, or the publication of a report and even, in certain circumstances, the outcome of a court case.

The local angle

Of course, there are other ways of raising the relevance or topicality of a news item or a feature. One of these is to localize it, as in the case of the Bristol & West Building Society mentioned earlier, so that quotes are attributable to a local manager or director. This has two benefits, the first being that a local angle is provided, making the item more likely to be used, and the second being the reminder to the reader, or if one is fortunate, the listener or viewer, that an organization has a local presence. It follows that such localized material is of greatest benefit to those organizations which might not automatically be considered to have a presence or an interest in a particular area. A bank or building society, for example, which by its name is linked to one part of the country, will find that localized material will remind people of its presence elsewhere, but this always assumes that the news or features items being provided are suitable for use in the first place. As mentioned in Chapter 4, not every product or service is suitable for promotion in this way, either due to a lack of public, and therefore media, interest, or because so many other companies are doing the same thing. The launch of a new type of mortgage or a savings account will often be of interest, and the arrival of a new model of a particular marque of car could be of interest, but many more usual household or similar products will have to be advertised.

Timing

The need to time the announcement of a major story so that it will have a better chance of being used or given due prominence is also important. It is pointless issuing a financial story late in the afternoon, when many financial journalists are clearing their stories for publication the following morning, and if it is a personal finance story, often Wednesday will be too late for publication on the following Saturday or Sunday. Newspapers do have journalists working into the small hours of the morning, revising layouts and writing new stories or up-dating stories first carried in earlier editions, but these are working on the major life and death stories, on accidents, crime, war, terrorism, or political intrigue. Most of the stories handled by the vast majority of PR people are not in this category – and that is perhaps something for which they can be truly thankful!

Breaking a story

There are two conflicting theories over the attitudes of the media as to when and how a story breaks.

The first of these is the safest for the PR practitioner who intends to remain on good terms with his or her employers or clients and the media over the longer term. This is to remember that the local weekly, morning daily, daily evening and Sunday newspapers all have different deadlines. A story which surfaces in the wrong newspaper at the wrong time can be paid less attention by other newspapers which see this as something which has broken elsewhere, if indeed they use it at all. Much depends on the importance of the story, and whether it is still developing so that something can be added to the original. Sunday newspapers hate following the Saturday newspapers, and daily newspapers feel the same about the relationship between their Monday edition and the Sunday newspapers. Certainly, any story which breaks in a Sunday newspaper will need to be very worthwhile indeed to appear again on the Monday morning, and nothing short of dramatic to appear in Monday's evening newspapers.

There in an alternative viewpoint that journalists under pressure are more concerned over missing a story than appearing to be following another newspaper. This is an altogether more hazardous and difficult course, but it results on occasion from the desperation for media coverage which one sometimes finds. The ploy is to offer the story as a 'scoop', in plain English a 'first', to a journalist. There are occasions when this can work, but usually, giving a journalist a scoop can be a dangerous strategy, since extra coverage in that journalist's newspaper might be at the expense of reasonable coverage elsewhere, as rival editors refuse to give the story sufficient attention as they too wish to be first, not second, with the news. This is one major difference between people in PR and those in journalism, since the ideal of every journalist is to write an exclusive story, while that of the PR person is to get as wide a coverage as possible. This doesn't matter too much with the routine product stories, which if handled with a reasonable degree of competence by those in media relations will at least appear on the specialized pages of the newspapers in the case of such things as personal finance, travel or motoring news.

It does happen sometimes, if the story really is important enough, that other newspapers and broadcasting stations will use a story which has broken elsewhere. The danger which then arises is that the journalists charged with writing the story will be looking for additional, more up-to-date information so that the story does not become a simple rewrite of the original. Apart from the nuisance value for the PR practitioners and their management or client being besieged by journalists looking for more information or even a 'new angle', the danger is that in their haste and determination to add to the original, they might produce something which is somewhat distorted. One influential Scottish morning newspaper missed an important financial story which was leaked and first appeared in a Sunday newspaper. The problem was compounded when the newspaper in question failed to cover the story on the Monday morning, and then on the Tuesday morning published a highly speculative story about a 'mole hunt' at the financial institution in question!

This is why the first course, that of ensuring as widespread a coverage as possible with the initial release of the story, is so important, and so much safer.

The one occasion when giving a journalist a scoop does have value arises when a particular journalist stumbles over a story before the organization is ready to announce it, or is able to announce it since contracts or other details might not have been finalized. The promise of being first to learn of the details will sometimes encourage the journalist in question to sit on the story and not publish until the eve of the formal announcement. Even so, one might be able to do better, by giving the journalist additional background so that when the story is released generally, his coverage can be better than that of his rivals, even though it appears on the same day.

Flooding the media with too many stories can be harmful, unless they are targeted for different journalists or different newspapers. No journalist is going to believe that the ACME Manufacturing Corporation has yet another splendid new product innovation every day for 30 or 40 days in succession. Public relations must have the authority to hold back or even abandon less important stories if there is a danger of flooding the media or distracting them from other more significant events within a particular organization. Quality is important, and more important than quantity. Preparing a story for the sake of having something to say is wrong and counter-productive, since anything without substance will be 'spiked'.

The emphasis on quality, and of not doing something simply for the sake of it, cannot be over-stressed. There are people in public relations, and especially in consultancy, who will programme a certain number of stories per month or over a year. The unwary user of PR, and especially the purchaser of PR consultancy services, is likely to be misled into selecting the wrong practitioner if one candidate claims to be able to issue a certain number of media releases or articles over a given period, while another simply suggests that they will be able to identify the right opportunities. Never confuse PR, and especially media relations, with advertising, where one can promise a certain number of media insertions.

IDENTIFYING OPPORTUNITIES

Most PR practitioners will be fortunate enough to have a ready-made supply of opportunities for media relations activities. The availability of these opportunities will vary. On some occasions, two or three stories might appear almost simultaneously, while at other times opportunities might be few and far between. It is important to understand exactly what can be used, its timing, and the likely target media. The need to be proactive and ever vigilant for such opportunities is essential since, as mentioned in the previous chapter, for every manager who believes that his or her pet project deserves the front page, there is another who hasn't realized the significance of what is happening, or only considers the possibility of media relations when it is too late to organize any which is truly effective.

Planning

There are those who believe that media relations is flexible and can respond quickly, and there are many occasions when this is absolutely right. Often out of necessity, a good press office can prepare and distribute a media release in an extremely short time, or even organize and convene a press conference or briefing at short notice. In extremes, a short press release can be written and distributed within 20 minutes or less. A press conference can be convened within an hour or so. Yet, such action is normally reactive, and most often reflects the needs of crisis management. The ability of the media to respond, using the press release or ensuring that a reporter turns up at the press conference at such short notice, reflects the significance of the event and the fact that they are already interested in the story.

The truth is that preparation and planning give media relations a far better chance of success. In the case of the launch of a product, there is sufficient time for the launch to be well coordinated, with dealers or distributors briefed, goods in stock, advertising campaigns prepared so that they can follow and not pre-empt news and features coverage in the media, and timing can be just right so that specialized features pages, which are often prepared in advance, can cover the development. If the release relates to an item of research, journalists can have the extra time necessary to prepare a more extensive story, perhaps obtaining a more thorough background briefing, or having the time to follow particular angles to the story which will interest their readers.

A common mistake is to provide too much information or too little, since a newspaper needs enough and no more. Too little information means leaving questions unanswered, while too much means treating newspapers and their stories as if they were detailed contracts or specification documents, and forgetting the whole purpose of journalism, which is to keep the audience informed and entertained, and certainly never bored. Of course, often by 'too much' one is referring not to a surfeit of detailed information, but instead to too much padding, just as 'too little' might not mean an unduly short press release or article, but vague and meaningless writing.

There is no correct length for a press release – the correct length is as short as it is possible to be while covering the necessary facts, and perhaps adding a comment which humanizes the piece, as well as, in the best examples, adding information which is best handled through a comment or quote than in the main body of the text.

Opportunities for coverage

So, what are the opportunities for media coverage with which we should concern ourselves? The answer is that any opportunity should be considered, and the full extent to which the story can be exploited should be examined.

The most obvious instances when media coverage will be possible include:

- New or improved products or services.

- Major contracts, especially export contracts, including those which take the company or its product into a new market, and those which will create employment or at least ensure job security for existing employees.

- In the case of specialized publications, new promotional efforts, such as advertising campaigns, new packaging, promotional activities, and competitions, although prize-winners are only usually suitable for coverage in the local newspaper in their home town.

- Production milestones or other measures of success, such as the millionth car off the production line, or the two-millionth passenger on a ship.

- Relevant statistics are often of general interest, such as details of property prices, bank lending, agricultural output, and so on.

- Major sponsorships, especially if the cost can be revealed since the larger the sum, the greater the news value.

- The results of research conducted by your organization, especially if you are prepared to commit yourselves to making forecasts or can identify a trend, or better still, a change in an earlier trend.

- Appointments, even at branch level, since the interest will become more localized the less senior the position.

- VIP visits to factories, ships or installations, and even visits by local councillors or a local MP will be of interest to the local media.

- Orders for new equipment or the purchase of new premises, especially if this reflects the success of the business.

The extent to which any story can be guaranteed coverage is dependent on two factors beyond the control of the media relations specialists, no matter how good they might be. The first is the quality of the story itself, but one can do much to improve this; while the second is the pressure on the news or features space of the target publications and broadcasting stations. The specialized trade publications are less prone to this problem than the more general media, but even so it can happen that several companies in a particular sector launch new products at the same time, and it is impossible to provide the same editorial coverage for each of them within a finite number of editorial pages. It is extremely difficult, and sometimes impossible, for a newspaper publisher to increase the number of pages at short notice, and it is even more difficult for a specialized publication to do this. Unless additional advertising can be obtained to support the additional pages, the viability of the publication will be undermined, and even if the advertising sales team feel that they can do this, at short notice and without heavy discounting, the printer might not be able to cope. Distribution costs can also rise sharply if the publication becomes heavier.

Ideally, one should always examine copies of publications in which your organization or your client is likely to be interested, but this is not always possible or practical at short notice. Good reference books offer a reasonably safe short cut, as we will see in the next chapter.

As already mentioned in Chapter 1, one opportunity which must never be overlooked in any attempt to obtain the maximum media coverage is what may be best be described as the seasonal opportunity. This includes Christmas, the January interest in package holidays, and the spring wedding season. The fashion trade is perhaps most highly geared to seasonal opportunities, and most aware of one of the major requirements of PR activity in support of seasonal opportunities – advance preparation. It is no use drawing a magazine editor's attention to the worthy goods produced by your company or by your client in early December when many magazines prepare their Christmas special features as early as August. Again, if one wants to take travel writers abroad to sample your company's holidays or travel services, this will need to be done outside the peak months when demand from paying customers will be highest, but a late autumn press trip will not bear fruit until the following January or February in many cases.

It is vital, when working so far ahead, to ensure that accurate information on prices and availability should be available as far in advance as possible. Newspaper journalists can often change their 'copy' at relatively short notice, and so a diary note to keep in touch will be useful, but magazines are far more difficult, and good advance awareness of the situation at publication time will be essential to success. One should be in no doubt at all that a major failure or change will embarrass the journalist and the publication, and will make them wary of mentioning your company or its products in future.

FOLLOW-UP ACTIVITY

Once a major announcement has been made or a major development publicized, there will often be opportunities to capitalize on the impact of the story. Sometimes, such follow-up activity gains extra significance, if the original story did not attract the attention it may have deserved, for example.

One good example of what can happen arose when a major shipping and road haulage company announced plans some years ago to introduce a new integrated road haulage and ferry service to Northern Ireland. As inevitably happens, stories such as this are more important 'offshore' than on the mainland, and the initial announcement attracted widespread media interest, with the broadcasting stations in Northern Ireland especially interested in interviews. The scale of the investment added to the interest, as is usually the case when a story involves an area with a relatively weak economy. Yet, in spite of this, the actual inauguration of the service had less impact, even though the presence of a new ship and a naming ceremony added visual interest. This was simply because the event coincided with the start of negotiations on the political future of Northern Ireland, and newspaper photographers and television cameramen were required elsewhere. The initial sailing of the first ship was shown briefly on the late night local news bulletin on just one of the two available television stations, and less newspaper space was obtained than might have been the case otherwise. To ensure that key audiences were aware that the service was operating, a series of 'follow-up' stories were run on large or interesting loads, which would previously have required specially chartered shipping for successful movement. Many of these were visually interesting, and were often released as 'photo-caption' stories.

Angles

There are those who believe that it is difficult to have more than one piece of good coverage for a particular development. This is sometimes the case, but it is possible to have different angles to a story and to obtain further coverage as a result. One good example of this arose when the Royal Bank of Scotland opened a new office in Gibraltar. Opinions on the way in which the story should be handled varied, with one PR consultant advising that nothing should be done until the official opening of the office, scheduled for some two months after the real opening. The view taken in-house, and accepted by the management, was that this was wrong. The prominent position of the new office meant that it could not be ignored, and media interest would be lost if they felt that it had been open for some time. The interest of the story was more than a simple bank branch opening, since it reflected both the growing status of Gibraltar as an offshore financial centre, and the European aspirations of a Scottish bank, which was operating the branch in conjunction with its Spanish partner as the first joint venture in Gibraltar between a British and a Spanish business.

The opening of the office for business by the Chief Minister for Gibraltar received coverage not just in the local media, but also in the quality London and Scottish newspapers, and in a number of media targeted at expatriates. The formal opening two months later, with the chairmen of the Scottish and Spanish banks present, also received coverage. The difference was that the initial coverage centred on the status of Gibraltar as an offshore financial centre, and the second concentrated on the joint venture aspects of the story.

Budget follow-up

Even the more topical stories can benefit from follow-up activity. A good example is the annual Budget statement by the Chancellor of the Exchequer, which each year provides an opportunity for many organizations to predict the Chancellor's actions, or to lobby for special attention to be given to a particular activity or area of need. The extent to which any one organization can do this will depend on their business or other activity and the likely relevance of the Budget to this. Nevertheless, if one assumes that the Budget statement is relevant to the organization, and that comment from it would not be out of place, the activity could consist of:

1. A month or so before the Budget statement, a press release highlighting the main points contained in and accompanying a paper on the Budget, and commentary on what could or should be done. In the case of a financial institution, the paper could extend to including an analysis of the Chancellor's options.

2. The press release should be followed by articles on the Budget featuring the likely measures which a senior member of the organization's board or management expects, and why.

3. On Budget afternoon, an instant two or three paragraph reaction to the Budget measures should be released to the media once the Chancellor has concluded his main points. Advance preparation of half-a-dozen or so reactions, featuring the most likely measures, makes this possible in the tight timescale. The use of facsimile services will be essential to success, and this can also be helped by using the wire services of Two-Ten Communications.

4. The following day, if any particular measure is relevant to the organization's activities, a more considered analysis can be released, ideally picking up points which will have escaped the general run of comment and instant reaction in the previous evening's broadcast news programmes, and the morning's newspapers.

5. If thorough analysis shows a major impact on a particular market or a particular section of the community, this can be released later, but not too much later.

One financial institution managed all of these stages following one Budget which withdrew tax relief on home improvement loans, with the final comment making dire predictions for the future condition of the nation's housing stock! Usually, one should be content to achieve items 1 to 3.

Follow-up features

Trade press features follow-up for a major story is also important. The trade press are often interested in customer case studies, although the length and treatment may vary widely, with some looking for an extensive article while others basically require a good photograph and a caption.

Articles on topics of interest written by directors or senior management will often be used, and on occasion, these might be of interest to more general publications as well as the specialized press. Such articles often cost less to prepare than case studies, and can usually be prepared in far less time. After all, a good case study requires identification of a customer, and the customer's cooperation. A case study with a number of photographs can easily require the customer, or one of his senior managers, to spend half a day or so with the person writing the article and the photographer. The customer will also have to be offered the chance of vetting the article, which takes more time. Fortunately, satisfied customers are usually happy to cooperate, realising that some of the glory reflects on them and their business.

After all this, often the article by a director or senior manager will raise more interest in the trade press, and in those cases where reader response cards are provided, the article often provides a better response than the case study.

Articles and case studies must be written to the length specified by the editor of the publication. If it is too long and if the editor has time, the article will be edited, and the part which might be cut could be that which the author of the piece would have wished to see published. If the editor, or his sub-editors, haven't time, then the article will not be used. Newspapers and magazines know what they want, and often have their own idea of the 'natural' length for an article. Sometimes, they will use articles of varying lengths, but when an article is requested or commissioned, a length is mentioned because the editor or his features editor will have some idea of exactly how the article will be used. Local and regional newspapers will usually regard 500-600 words as a reasonable length, while the quality newspapers will go for 800–1200 words, and trade, professional and other specialized periodicals will differ in their requirements.

If an article has to be translated for use in a foreign language publication, it is worth bearing in mind that English is a comparatively concise language; French tends to be about 10 per cent longer, Spanish is slightly longer still, and German is some 15-20 per cent longer. There is more than a grain of truth in jests about the 'hat of my aunt', or 'the French have a word for it, the Germans have a sentence!'

Follow-up interviews

Of course, far better still than 'ghost-writing' an article oneself under the name of a director, or whatever, is to have the individual concerned interviewed by a journalist from the newspaper concerned, or indeed, to have a radio or television interview. This does require preparation of the person who is being interviewed, but even more important, the time or space for such interviews is limited, and these can only be provided when the publication or the broadcasting station feels that there is something of interest for their audience. The decision to ask for an interview belongs to the media, not to the PR practitioner, although one can do something to arouse their interest. Broadcast interviews especially are reactive, usually following a major announcement or other development covered in a news programme. Regular television documentary or features programmes, such as the Money Programme, will select a topic of current interest, and then identify suitable interviewees who they feel will be able to talk with authority and interview easily and professionally.

As already mentioned in the previous chapter, it is often essential to arrange media training for those likely to be interviewed frequently by the media. Media training is best conducted away from the office using specialist consultancies who can arrange a realistic studio setting, and also use experienced broadcasting or newspaper journalists, ideally with some knowledge of the trainee's business or profession.

There are occasions when one can improve the coverage of a story. For example, if a subject lends itself to a good photograph, supplying this can help increase the amount of space obtained in those newspapers who didn't have a photographer available at the right time, or who couldn't justify sending a staff photographer. Providing television stations, and especially regional television stations, with a broadcast standard video containing some background material and an interview with a relevant expert or a director, can also improve the coverage given on television news. Even so, the news editor handling television is likely to be looking for 30 seconds or so of footage, and so vast quantities of material will hinder, rather than help him. In supplying any visual material, be it a photograph or video material, one must remember that editors will not want anything which smacks of advertising, and that company names, and especially brand names, are taboo to many.

THE ROUTINE

Not all news has to be good news. In some industries, price cuts or special offers, often forced by competition or poor demand, will be announced, but never price rises! Transport operators are accustomed to announcing fare increases, partly because in some cases these have to be applied for and approved by the regulatory authorities. Motor vehicle manufacturers are also well to the fore in announcing price increases, while financial institutions announce changes to interest rates, but there are still many businesses which resist announcing increases. The failure to do so is understandable in those industries, such as construction, aircraft manufacturing and shipbuilding, where individual orders are negotiated separately and variations on the standard product are such as to render a price list unnecessary. For the remainder, announcing price increases would not only appear to be professional and honest, but it would achieve two other aims; the first being to raise name awareness and the second being to stimulate demand for existing stocks. There is a further possibility, that of explaining why an increase is required, and that in turn lends itself to establishing the company as one prepared to speak on industry topics. It takes time to become one of the media's favoured industry spokespersons, and no opportunity to build this reputation should be missed.

CHECKLIST

- What are the annual or seasonal opportunities which your organization offers?

- Ensure that new products or the launch of new campaigns are accompanied by a timetable and an agreed action plan, so that opportunities can be identified and prepared for.

- Consider who should speak for your organization and ensure that they are properly trained, well enough in advance to avoid any panic, but not so far ahead that training loses its relevance.

7

Reaching the Media

Media relations is of fundamental importance to any public relations programme, but we have already seen how badly media relations is often conducted. Many will argue that the fault does not always lie with the public relations practitioner, and blame either those in another management discipline or perhaps the culture of the organization for poor relations with and indifferent handling of the media. There are, it is true, those organizations which do not understand the media, and either will not talk to journalists or will do so only when it suits their purposes. Everyone has an example of the individual who is happy to discuss the good news about his or her organization, or his or her career, but refuses to deal with the bad. On the other hand, it is the role of the public relations practitioner to advise and this means counselling one's colleagues or clients on the importance of dealing with the media. In common with every other aspect of public relations, media relations should not be a series of ad hoc exercises, but a sustained programme. Times of difficulty or crisis make effective communication more important, rather than less, and journalists, and those who follow their work, have greater respect for managements able to communicate effectively and openly at all times.

Effective media relations require the public relations practitioner to consider four major aspects of their role, which can be broadly and briefly summarized as follows:

1. Establishing a policy on media relations for the organization. This is the most important aspect of the role, since everything else flows from it, and includes such matters as who can and who can't talk to the media.

2. Handling the issue of material to the media.

3. Media distribution lists, which are so often neglected.

4.   Planning and organization of media events.

As mentioned in Chapter 5, it is also important that the client or one's employer, or colleagues since many will be at the same level as the practitioner, are aware of the correct terminology or jargon for their contact with the media, with suitable training for those who need it.

MEDIA RELATIONS POLICY

Attitudes to media contact vary enormously, and so too do the reasons. There are, of course, those directors and managers who welcome it, and take great pleasure in a high profile and will accord the highest priority to visits to broadcasting studios, and will make themselves available so that journalists of all kinds can have the benefit of their wisdom. This is one extreme. The other extreme consists of those who will go to any length and make any excuse to avoid meeting, or even talking over the telephone to, a journalist. Topics become 'too trivial', or there is a risk of 'giving away information to our competitors', or the belief that whatever is said will be 'distorted by the media – they always get these things wrong!'

As with most things, there is a balance to be achieved. Courting the media unnecessarily risks disaster if it is taken too far, especially if this happens to be in pursuit of the cult of the individual. It is also unwise to approach the media pretending to have something of interest for them; journalists are almost invariably able to see whether or not there is a story. On the other hand, simply meeting a journalist or journalists with whom one is likely to have future dealings to establish contact at an early stage is usually welcomed. Ignoring the media, or even hiding from them, risks being overlooked or becoming suspect in their eyes. Certainly, opportunities can be lost, and security is seldom a suitable excuse since in most industries, one will find that one's competitors know your business better than the media do. Journalists get their stories right more often than they get them wrong, but, of course, cannot be expected to bore their readers, listeners or viewers with unnecessary detail. Significantly, journalists who can speak to those with first hand knowledge produce a better and more accurate story than those who have to scrape around for information from whatever source might be available. Let it also be said, that the best journalists have a high standard of ethics, and will keep information to themselves if they know that it is confidential and simply given to them so that they do not draw the wrong conclusions from the information more generally available – in short, a truly professional journalist with a pride in his work appreciates anyone who helps him or her to maintain a reputation for accuracy and perception.

Who talks to the media?

The wise businessman, politician, organizer or leader of a charity or pressure group, trade association or trade union, will make himself or herself readily accessible to the media, and aim to be sufficiently well respected by the media to have due notice given to his or her opinions. The individual in question is most likely to be the boss, in business terms the chairman or chief executive, but could also be the finance director or other specialized senior manager who could emerge as a leading spokesman on the way in which a particular development will affect the industry, charity, or whatever. One can delegate the freedom to talk to the media, and should do so. For media contact, the ability and accessibility of directors and senior specialists does not eliminate the need for professional PR advisers, but rather enables them to be more effective, since they should be monitoring contacts and sitting in on interviews whenever possible. Being present at an interview also improves the PR practitioner's knowledge and their subsequent ability to act as a spokesperson whenever the directors are absent.

Obviously, such an approachable organization will have first had to review its policies over the disclosure of information, and decide just which of its management team can be allowed to talk to the media, and the limits of their authority to talk. This is another reason why the professional PR adviser is so important. Generally, the chairman, chief executive and finance director are the three most important individuals in media terms, but their deputies are also acceptable substitutes provided that this does not happen too often. Nevertheless, there are others who should also be considered, and these include:

- Heads of specialized departments, as already mentioned, so that the media can have specialized briefings or interview someone with direct knowledge and experience of the subject in hand. A journalist following a railway story might wish to speak to the chief civil engineer or the chief signals engineer, for example.

- The local manager, both to provide local interest and because of his or her understanding of the situation in their area.

- The person on the spot, perhaps the senior police officer or fire officer at a disaster, or a relief worker 'in the field' providing support in an area affected by famine, for example.

- The person doing the actual job, such as a train driver or a surgeon, who can talk about their perceptions of an event or activity.

Your organization or your client may have others to add to this list. The point is that the media need to humanize the story, and they also lack, as individuals, first hand experience of almost anything other than their own profession, something which they share with politicians and investment analysts, teachers and the clergy, amongst others. The less senior people are, the less confident they will feel about dealing with the media, and the more important it is that they have a briefing by public relations specialists before an interview, and ideally have the benefit of a PR presence during the interview.

The PR role

Indeed, one has to consider carefully the role of PR in dealing with the media, and for that matter, in doing so, one is also looking at the place of PR people in handling other groups, such as pressure groups, investment analysts and so on. It is important that the PR function has the credibility to do more than simply channel media enquiries to specialist line managers, on the one hand, while on the other, it is equally important not to make the mistake of leaving the PR function to handle all enquiries, without the opportunity of offering the media an expert opinion.

Journalists, and less frequently, investment analysts will often be happy to talk to a PR person who has the authority to speak with confidence, and has both a good level of knowledge and an understanding of the organization's activities and that of others in the same field. The role of the PR person is that of handling enquiries, providing information and, if he or she is really good, often discussing the background to a particular development, in addition to facilitating and arranging interviews between management and the media. A great deal of interruption and general management time can be saved if the PR function has the necessary expertise and authority to be able to handle more than 90 per cent of media enquiries, while the PR function and the media concerned with a particular subject develop close ties. Needless to say, such a PR function knows exactly what particular journalists will find of interest.

At the same time, a good newspaper story often works even better if a quote is deliberately attributed to a key figure in an organization or an industry. One can sometimes get round this by agreeing a quote, which can then be made available to the media, but individual newspapers and journalists have their own way of asking questions, and might be more interested in one aspect of a particular development, and less interested in another, so this is a somewhat inflexible approach. It also has limitations with broadcasting, for while one can prepare such things as a 'video news release', so that television stations have a recorded interview or background information available when the news breaks, they will also appreciate being able to ask their own questions and develop those aspects of the story which appeal most to their viewers.

The dividing line between what management can say, and what can be left to the PR function is a hazy one, and it will depend on the quality of spokespeople available.

Using PR to sift requests for interviews by the media has a number of advantages, not the least of which is that time will not be wasted unnecessarily and contact will be between the journalists and management who are most suited on a particular topic. The PR function should first clearly identify the topic or topics which the journalist wishes to discuss, and also provide a short briefing on both this and, if possible, the journalist involved, doing this verbally if time is short. There is no point in the interviewee taking a superficial approach with a good specialized journalist, or being too technical with someone writing for the general popular press. Ideally, a PR person should be present at all meetings with the media, and there are several reasons for this as follows:

1. The PR person can provide guidance and support. This will depend on the person being interviewed, but a relatively junior member of the management team, or one who has had little contact with the media, will need careful guidance on what can and can't be said. A specialist, or someone whose authority covers a particular activity, will find the PR person's broader, but necessarily shallower, knowledge of the wider organization to be a useful complement to his own knowledge.

2. The PR person can ensure that the rules for what can and can't be quoted will be followed by *both* parties.

3. Interviews, especially with senior people, act as a briefing for the PR function, updating them on what is going on, and also on just how far the organization is prepared to be quoted on a development. Even in organizations with good PR briefing and PR 'sitting in' on committees and management meetings, there is nothing like a good interview, with questions and answers, to draw out the full story.

4. PR ensures fair play for both parties, avoiding embarrassing letters to the editor to the effect that someone or other 'didn't say that'.

5. The PR people may have some tidying up to do! This is not unusual and doesn't reflect any discredit on the organization. What happens is that a journalist will discover during the interview that he or she needs some particular item, perhaps a photograph, a copy of an old annual report, or some detailed statistics which couldn't have been foreseen. The PR person has the task of ensuring that whatever might be needed is found and sent to the journalist as quickly as possible.

6. PR people understand the jargon of journalism and the jargon of the industry for which they are working. Jargon isn't really good practice, but to be realistic, it is part of modern life, and it does help to have an 'interpreter' present. Different modes of transport have different jargon, and there are even different terms between, for example, banks and building societies. Specialist journalists will be familiar with such terms, but there will be newcomers and generalists, so one should never assume familiarity.

MEDIA RELEASES

As mentioned earlier, most still refer to press releases and in reality few people use the term 'media release'. Possibly the term will never really become accepted. One can take some comfort that such adherence to inaccurate and out-dated terms is not the preserve of public relations or marketing since, after all, one still hears of ships 'sailing', almost two centuries after the advent of the steamship!

Press releases, news release or, in government circles, press notices are one of the essential ingredients of media relations activity. Good media relations will not come by good press releases alone, but they are a start, and as important as a good letter of application for a job. Sometimes press releases will be run in their entirety by a newspaper, but this is rare. This can be seen as a compliment to the writer of the release, but most often, it is a reflection on the publication concerned, whose journalists are either under too much pressure, or too lazy or, in some cases in the poorer trade publications and the worst examples of local freesheets, too unprofessional to concern themselves with recasting the story to fit the interests and attention span of their readers. Of course, the better drafted a press release is, the more likely it is to survive intact, but some poor releases also receive unedited attention! There is one regional daily newspaper which not only fails to edit press releases, but rather than cut the release to whatever length can be accommodated, simply reduces the size of type to ensure that nothing is missed!

It is important that releases are used solely for something which is newsworthy and not for information which might be suitable for the features page, but which is certainly not new, and not news.

The basic rules for drafting a press release were covered in Chapter 5, but never forget there is a balance to be obtained between providing too little information and too much. Insufficient detail will hamper good communications as the media either fail to have their interest aroused or find the time and trouble of the follow-up telephone call too tiresome. It might even be that the telephone lines to the press office will be jammed, so many cannot get through! Leaving too much to the follow-up enquiries by journalists also means that consistency of communication is not achieved. On the other hand, too much is indigestible. While journalists will follow up a story to find their own angle or to obtain additional information, always be open to the possibility of producing more than one version of the press release for different media. For example, a new cruise liner will have a different interest to the general press compared to the shipping press, and in the town where the ship is to be built, the story will be about jobs. At the same time the financial press may be interested in the cost and the investment implications. Time sometimes makes this targeting difficult, but if it is worth doing and time is available, the impact is that much greater. The difficulty of serving these different audiences is often exaggerated, since the headline and the first paragraph are the two elements likely to be changed with the main part of the release being the same for all audiences.

Video news releases

While the most important stories of widespread general interest will be reported on television and the television stations will happily send a reporter and a news gathering team, there are a number of occasions, especially on regional television, where resources are often limited and the story is not quite important enough for a news gathering team to be sent. The solution to this is the so-called 'video news release', which is a short report or an interview on the subject. This provides added visual impact so that the story is not simply reported, and because television is obviously a visual medium, the presence of good video footage might make a difference between the story being covered or dropped. Video news releases must be on broadcast standard tape for easy use and to assist editing by the television station. Some video production companies specialize in this service and the best of them often have direct lines to the major television stations so that material can be transmitted immediately and in useable form. Relatively little of the material recorded by a television or radio interviewer will be used, and one is often fortunate to have just a 30 second mention, so never be disappointed if the carefully constructed interview appears as a brief comment.

Follow-up

It can sometimes be helpful to have a follow-up feature available for any publication which requires additional information, but this is usually far more important for trade and technical developments than for the general run of consumer news. Local newspapers, faced with a press release on a new branch, might run it, depending on how significant it is to the area in question, but a follow-up article might need advertising support to be used. Much depends on the quality, of course, and the degree of interest. The most interesting and newsworthy developments will be followed up by the features writers, anxious to provide their readers with the background to a major development.

MEDIA LISTS

It is probably seeking the impossible to find a media list which is entirely up-to-date. Apart from the appearance and disappearance of publications and the growth in the number of broadcasting stations, journalists do move to new jobs. Nevertheless, finding media lists which are badly out-of-date, with perhaps a third or more of the specialized correspondents or even the media themselves no longer as recorded, cannot be excused.

On joining one company, the author asked to see their media distribution list, and found just one large list for every type of publication likely to be interested in the company and its products. The company's products were those of interest to consumers and to businesses, while there was the added dimension of the city correspondents given the company's listing on the London Stock Exchange. The secretary handling the mailing list did not know whether a particular press release was intended for everyone or just a few of the publications on the list, so everyone got everything. Apart from the cost in postage and stationery, the result was that journalists found so little of interest to them each time, that even the potentially worthwhile releases were thrown straight into the waste paper bin.

Most organizations can divide their mailing list into several categories, differentiating between audiences. A charity might find this difficult, but businesses can often distinguish between personal, or consumer, and business products; between news on the company and its financial performance, and technical stories; and between local, regional, national and international news. In a reasonably broadly-based or diversified company, several lists might be necessary, and a dozen or more would not be uncommon.

Distribution

Attention has also to be paid to the physical act of distribution. Should one use the mail, couriers, the facsimile machine or a wire service? The mail is inexpensive, although one has to build an extra day into the timing of the release, especially if deadlines have to be observed. Couriers are expensive, and really only viable if a substantial number of addresses have to be reached within a given area. The facsimile machine is useful, but at busy periods numbers are often engaged, and in the shambles of the typical newspaper office, pages become separated and lost. Wire services, of which the one most commonly used by PR practitioners is that operated by Two-Ten Communications (the former UNS), provide a rapid response service well suited to the immediacy of much news output, but can never target as carefully as one's own list can. The use of Two-Ten's wire service is, nevertheless, one way around the problem of the permanently engaged telephone line. Telephoning every publication and asking for the copy taker, and then dictating material, is not always successful, and will only be available to the better respected organizations. Some newspapers sift requests by outsiders to be allowed to dictate copy, using the news editor or a suitable specialized correspondent and only on their recommendation will the copy taker accept a telephone call. Apart from dictating copy to Two-Ten, or sending it using a facsimile machine, one can also establish a data link so that copy goes straight into their own computers: this is the fastest and most accurate means of sending copy to Two-Ten.

Worthwhile material will also be accepted by the PA or Reuters wire services, but one has to remember that Reuters and PA themselves make an editorial judgement on a story and write it to suit their subscribers (the media), while Two-Ten is working for the organizations issuing the story. On the other hand, because they are independent and working for the newspapers rather than for the companies issuing stories, Reuters and PA material has an extremely high acceptance rate and many newspapers will not bother to rewrite the story. The same can be said for other major wire services, such as AP-Dow Jones and Extel.

Using the list

Addressing material to a named contact on a newspaper or at a broadcasting station is invaluable, especially if one is assured that he or she will be on duty at their office on the day. Otherwise, one should also let their departmental editor have a copy as well, in case they are absent.

The correspondent system means that one can identify those journalists most likely to be interested in your organization, but there will always be occasions when an unknown journalist stands in for the named correspondent, and perfection in targeting media releases becomes difficult to achieve.

One can also compile one's own lists from the *PR Planner*, a loose-leaf reference publication which is up-dated frequently. A computerized variant on the *PR Planner* is *PR Targeter*, and in addition to their own set lists or lists which can be compiled quickly on an ad hoc basis, there is scope for compiling one's own standing lists, although, at present, the computer's own automatic up-dating service does not reach the standing lists. Sometimes journalists will telephone or write, asking to be included on a company's mailing list, and, of course, one can also add those whose names are seen on newspaper articles about your sector or activity.

Finally, ône should never forget those freelance journalists who cover your specialization, many of whom are worth half-a-dozen staff reporters or writers to a PR person.

Liaison with journalists

There are those in PR who firmly believe that one can draw a comparison between media relations and selling, inasmuch as the media become the customers or clients. To take this further, one can quote the old adage about the best bargains being those which leave both parties pleased, taking place between a willing vendor and a willing purchaser, and even today, it is unduly cynical to suggest that such happy transactions no longer exist. On the other hand, one should not treat journalists as if one is selling to them! A hard sell technique could rebound upon the 'salesman', and so it should.

There is another big difference between selling and media relations. In business, monopoly situations can arise either through genuine innovation, the failure of a competitor, or other circumstances in which the market can only bear one supplier of a certain type of goods or services. Objectivity and the need to be seen as independent, means that the media cannot accept a single supplier of information. Journalists will contact your competitors for a quote or for information. Occasionally, a company which does little to engender good media relations might seem to obtain coverage out of proportion when something is done or is said, simply to avoid the media concerned being regarded as being in the pockets of those who do so much to ensure a constant and consistent flow of information.

It is always worthwhile, if the story is important, alerting your main contacts to the fact that it is coming, so that they will be either expecting the story or able to forewarn you if they are likely to be absent. Most newspaper offices operate in a state of some confusion and perhaps even a little anarchy. On one major provincial morning newspaper, journalists like to be standing by the facsimile machine waiting for their messages, or at least warned to hunt through the 'in-tray' for them, since the machine is located by the newsroom of their sister evening newspaper, whose journalists not only 're-direct' stories of interest, but also tend to toss uninteresting stories or material not meant for them to the side or even into the waste paper basket. Of course, most journalists, in the midst of writing a story, hate being interrupted by press officers asking whether or not they have received a story 'sent last week', so please, before telephoning and making a nuisance of yourself, do ask yourself the question: Is the story really that important? If it is, and you know and have a good relationship with your press contact, all will be well!

MEDIA EVENTS

The main media events of relevance to the public relations practitioner are as follows:

Press conferences

Press conferences are ideal for major events, which might include announcing details of a crisis, demonstrating a major new product, or announcing the financial results of a major company. Most new products, however, are not significant enough. Never use a conference to criticize a media story – on one occasion, a ferry company called a press conference to denounce and correct a story run on a television current affairs programme, only to find just two journalists turned up.

In practice, never have a press conference unless it is unavoidable or you really are sure that the event is important enough. If only a few journalists turn up to a press conference which proves to be of no value to them, rest assured, they won't make the same mistake twice.

Major publicly quoted companies often arrange press conferences following the announcement of their results – and do the same for investment analysts – but it is important to have the conference for the analysts first, simply because many financial journalists leave the press conference, and the first thing they do on returning to their office, before writing their stories is to consult their favourite analyst for an impartial 'city' opinion.

Press receptions

A cross between lunches and press conferences, receptions are a good idea if the news story is not strong enough, but one can field sufficient senior directors and managers for the press to feel that attendance and the opportunity for an informal discussion with leading figures in the organization is worthwhile.

Press lunches

Occasional press lunches are useful if linked to an interview or an opportunity to meet senior members of a management team. While the ideal is one journalist meeting one or two members of the management team, plus the PR person, journalists will attend lunches with other journalists present on condition that they know about this arrangement in advance, and it enables them to meet senior management or directors of sufficient worth – such lunches establish contact, and shouldn't be expected to achieve more than that.

Organization

In organizing any of these functions, remember the following:

1. Only select and invite those journalists who really are likely to be interested.

2. It is possible to refine point 1 above, simply by letting journalists know in broad terms what is on offer, and why.

3. Telephone 24 hours before the event to remind the guests and ensure that they are still interested.

4. Sign in all guests so that there is a record of who attended.

5. Brief the hosts in advance on who is attending, and on any likely issues or interests.

6. Only have hosts who have a strong sense of discretion, avoiding salesmen who will see this as an opportunity to sell to journalists who are touchy about their position of privilege and impartiality. One sales manager welcomed dealers and press to a product launch, and told the dealers that the press were present so that they would give the product plenty of coverage (something which nearly didn't happen).

7. There should be a programme, with a starting time, perhaps with coffee or pre-meal drinks (depending on the time of day), a time for the function itself to start, and a finishing time, which for lunch should be no later than 2.30 pm, so that busy journalists can get away.

8. Journalists unable to attend should have any material distributed at the function sent to them, both as a courtesy and for information.

9. Ensure that the timing is convenient for the media. Those working on Sunday newspapers usually do not work on Mondays. Weekly trade and local newspapers appearing on Friday normally go to press on Wednesday, which is, as a result, a long and very busy day for the journalists involved.

10. If at all possible, attempt to avoid clashing with another function of interest to the same journalists. It is not unknown for companies to deliberately attempt to compete with their rivals in this way, but it really is counter-productive or just plain silly to do so.

A sense of realism is necessary. One charity organized a function for its departing director-general, and the press, rightly, commented on the high quality of the champagne and the quantities available! Behaviour which is acceptable for a highly successful business is out of place for those seeking public largesse, either by voluntary donations or from the taxpayer. Never overdo the hospitality if the company is on the verge of bankruptcy!

We covered the appropriate terminology, or jargon, for media interviews in Chapter 5. It is important when speaking to anyone from the media to understand the terminology, and to preface remarks with the appropriate condition, rather than talking for half-an-hour or so, and then suggesting that everything is 'off-the-record' and should not be used! The journalist who will have been busily scribbling a record of the conversation will not be amused. Everything is on the record and likely to be used unless one says otherwise in advance and has the agreement of the journalist.

As we saw earlier, an embargo can be used to restrict publication or broadcast before a certain time and date. It can be useful, allowing journalists to research and write their story in advance, especially if there are complex issues involved. It can also enable a story to be timed for the greatest impact. Charities and pressure groups often time their material for release using the embargo system on a Monday morning, when newspapers will have been short of news and short of staff over the weekend, and so anxious for a good story and able to provide more space and a better position than usual. One can also time stories for a bank holiday week or for the bleak and difficult period between Christmas and the New Year.

The drawbacks of embargoed material are that one risks premature leaks, not so much because of newspapers or broadcasting stations breaking an embargo, which they are reluctant to do for fear of missing future material, but because competitors or rivals might be asked to respond to the story. Seeking comment from such sources enables the journalist to prepare and write a better story, which might suit your organization, or again, it might not. There is another danger. With one or two exceptions, even when sharing accommodation and within the same publishing organization, daily and Sunday newspapers have separate editorial teams, and so too do morning and evening newspapers, but often fax machines are shared. It simply takes a journalist from the 'wrong' newspaper to pick up the fax, and the story might appear on a Sunday rather than a Monday, or a Saturday rather than a Sunday, or in the previous evening's newspaper!

8

Making the Most of Photography

In Chapter 5, the value of photography in media relations and the way in which good photographic material can enhance media coverage was examined. Good photography does not occur by accident, and by 'good photography', one does not necessarily mean expensive photography. The society photographer charging £3000 or more a day is not the best person to photograph most new products, still less the inside of a busy factory or foundry, or even an office or retail premises. One can obtain good photography, and that means photographs editors are happy to use, at a much lower sum, often well below £1000 per day, with half-day or hourly rates also available.

The problems of obtaining good photography are not always fully appreciated, while its importance is sometimes treated too lightly. Good photography is not just technically correct, it has a creative aspect as well. The use of a good and highly professional photographer on a regular basis will often bring additional rewards, as the photographer comes to understand more about the organization and its products, and indeed, what it needs from photography.

Photography is a major responsibility of the public relations function, which will be expected to commission photography and maintain an adequate library of photographic material in almost any organization. Needless to say, its importance will vary between organizations. A firm of stockbrokers or accountants would make relatively little use of photographs, apart from a few of the head office and of senior partners, but a charity would need to be able to illustrate articles about its work, and indeed about those problems which it exists to solve. Commercial and military aircraft manufacturers will always have photographs on file which show aircraft on the production line and aircraft in the colour scheme or livery of each customer. Clothes manufacturers will have photographs of their products, and, of course, usually these will be photographs of the clothes being modelled. Package holiday operators will have photographs of the hotels featured in their brochures. These are just a few examples. Many businesses will need to have a good historical photographic library as well as covering current products, premises, customers or company personalities – the extent to which one will be expected to cover the past will vary between organizations and different sectors, but transport and travel, for both operators and manufacturers, and defence equipment, are all sectors in which there is a strong and continuing interest in history.

Essentially, photography is needed for the following applications:

1. To promote products or services and to make a story more likely to be used, perhaps ensuring a better position on the page of a newspaper or a magazine, or encouraging an editor to allocate extra space to the story. An editor once remarked to a PR person that the reason why that particular PR person's stories were always used was because the photography was always so good. There are limits, of course, since some products, particularly financial ones, cannot really be illustrated.

2. To announce and record an event, which could be anything from a VIP visit or factory opening, to the first flight of a new aeroplane, the first product from a new factory, the installation of new machinery, or an appointment.

3. To provide a record of the organization's progress and the way in which it will have changed over the years, its work, its achievements and its problems.

4. To enable the PR function to monitor application of the corporate identity – perhaps the only function which justifies PR people wandering around with cameras, since the results do not need to be of professional photographic standard.

5. To check on such matters as window displays, where standards can sometimes slip, and the interpretation of head office instructions can be misunderstood.

6. To illustrate products in use, especially to support case studies or provide additional material to illustrate features about the product.

THE IMPORTANCE OF GOOD PHOTOGRAPHY

Everyone knows the old adage about one good picture being worth a thousand words, but in media coverage terms, an illustration does rather more than that; it lifts the story and often will attract the attention of many who might not otherwise bother to read it. A colour illustration on a page of black and white (or monochrome) illustrations, also stands out. This has unfortunately caused a number of publications to ask media relations personnel to meet the cost of colour separations for printing of colour transparencies or prints, creating a difficult question over ethics. One should not pay for editorial coverage other than in an agreed advertorial, and photography is an aspect of editorial. While the publications in question are not the best in terms of quality, often they do have an important role to play, especially in the business-to-business and trade markets, and so the problem is not one which can be ignored. While a few PR practitioners have tried to curb the practice, they are, unfortunately, fighting a losing battle and it seems as if this unpleasant half-way house between 'free' editorial and 'paid-for' advertising will survive.

There are differences between PR and marketing over the way in which photography can be used, but PR must have control of the photography which it uses, be it for the annual report or employee communications, or, of course, for media use. The differences between the editorial style of photography which is most likely to be used by newspaper and magazine editors, and the advertising or brochure style favoured by marketing, can easily be seen if one examines a newspaper or magazine, looking first at the advertisements and then the news pages. Newspapers require something radically different from the advertising style favoured by marketing, and like to see products in action, rather than sitting either on their own or surrounded by adoring models!

Technical aspects

One should not overlook some of the more basic technical aspects of photography. Most newspapers and many magazines still print most of their photographs in monochrome, that is, black and white. Colour photographs printed in monochrome lack definition and contrast, often producing a 'fuzzy' or 'muddy' result. Good monochrome photography will provide a better result, and to allow the newspaper editorial staff the chance to reduce the photograph and retain quality, usually prints should be 8 by 6 inches, or even 10 by 8 inches, but portrait photographs can be as small as 5 by 4 inches.

Another reason why photographic prints should not be too small is that sometimes editors will wish to 'crop' a photograph before use. A head and shoulders portrait print might be reduced simply to a head, for example. At the time of considering contact prints ready for ordering enlargements, many commissioners of photography will also look for some careful cropping so that the impact of the photograph is heightened by the removal of any unnecessary detail or background material.

Despite advances in technology which have improved the quality of reproduction of colour in newspapers, there are still risks in providing colour prints since these do not always reproduce as well in colour as colour transparencies. Again, modern colour transparencies enlarge far more readily than those of even a few years ago, but there is still a chance of losing quality and crispness if a 35 mm transparency is used instead of a larger transparency of, say 2¼ inches square, if not larger still, especially if a whole page or cover illustration is to be the end result. One has to offset reproduction quality against practicality. If the photographer is working in a studio or in an easily accessible position, able to transport equipment easily, then there is the opportunity to use the right format (or size) of film. Unfortunately, the larger the format, the larger and heavier the camera, so a photographer asked to work in difficult, inaccessible and even dangerous conditions will need the lightest camera available, and will opt for 35mm.

Since printers also prefer colour originals to copy transparencies, it is useful if the photographer takes a substantial number of shots of each scene, and most will do this anyway, since often subtle differences in lighting or position will mean that out of 20 or 30 shots, one is noticeably better than all the rest. This is also true of black and white work. When photographing groups of people, there will always be those frustrating sessions when someone or other manages to blink every time, or glances in the wrong direction. This question of getting exactly the right angle for final use usually means that the photographer will provide a contact print for black and white or colour negative work, in which the developed film is laid on a sheet and small prints produced from which the photographer, the artistic director or the client choose the best material for enlargement. While one can look at transparencies through a light box and magnifier, sometimes a photographer will produce prints, and especially enlarged prints, to help his clients in selecting the right transparency for the printer.

Black and white photography normally uses 35mm film, since good enlargements from this small format are possible for most applications, and the camera is reasonably light and easy to handle, especially if the photography is conducted under difficult conditions.

If the story is truly of significance, it is a good idea to offer the news agencies the negatives so that they can produce copies for their subscribers.

Sometimes it is difficult to budget for photography for a year or so ahead because the PR function might not be fully aware of the extent of product development or the pace of new product launches. The solution to this problem is to ensure that the marketing department meets the cost of product photography for PR use, but this cannot absolve the PR department of responsibility for the direction of such photography. Simply expecting the marketing department to provide extra prints or transparencies is simply not enough to ensure good, newsworthy, photographic material.

Good product photos

Insufficient thought is sometimes given to using photography to make a point about a product. Sasco, the manufacturers of year planners, once used to simply issue to the trade media a photograph taken from the brochure for the coming year's planner range, and this accompanied a press release for the trade press so that office equipment dealers and stationers would order the product for their stock. Nothing was done to create interest among potential purchasers.

Photography played a major role in a new Sasco campaign aimed at raising awareness of the product among purchasers. Press releases were prepared for specific markets, such as industrial purchasers, professional practices such as doctors, dentists, veterinary surgeons, and so on, as well as for office publications. Quite simply the headline and first paragraph would mention a particular profession, along the lines of 'Planners help vets organize their practices in...' This was hardly the stuff of Shakespeare or Dickens, but it was useable enough. It worked because the photograph accompanying the press release showed a vet or doctor or dentist using a planner as appropriate. Preparation for this exercise was not too difficult or costly. Two models were used, one male and one female, who appeared in either their office clothes, white coats or brown coats, in a series of colour and black and white photographs. Office clothes enabled them to play a variety of roles, from sales managers through to clerical and secretarial workers. White coats meant that they could be described as vets, doctors, pharmacists and laboratory workers, while brown coats meant that they could be stock keepers or storeroom managers.

It is important when using models, who don't always have to be professionals, never to succumb to traditional concepts over who does what. Someone working in a kitchen doesn't have to be female and middle aged, while the manager giving dictation does not need to be male. People in photographs do not have to be white. As mentioned earlier, never ever put a naked girl into a photograph, unless it is relevant to the use of the product. One manufacturer of industrial showers used a naked girl in its trade advertising photographs, not because it reflected reality, but because it hoped that male purchasers would notice the advertisement. Such practices are frowned upon, and even if they do work in advertising, are unlikely to find editorial acceptance.

In case studies, using the customer or the employees of the customer is the ideal, but it is important that their approval is given. It helps if copies of the photographs are provided as souvenirs of the event, while some companies go further and either pay a small fee or provide a small gift as an acknowledgement of their assistance.

Making the most of photo-opportunities

Of course, opportunities to make the most of a story come about almost by chance, and it is important not to let such opportunities slip away. Sometimes, a good photograph will itself be the story, and words will never do the subject justice. Some years ago, for example, a company with extensive ship repairing interests had a ship in one of its dry docks ready for a major overhaul before being renamed and sold to Communist China. Part of the work included renaming the ship – a job which included lifting large Chinese characters onto the vessel and welding them into place. The idea of a massive steel Chinese character being lifted into place by a dockside crane appealed to the parent company's PR man, who telephoned the *Daily Telegraph* and suggested to the pictures editor that he might be interested in a photograph. The answer was 'yes, but only if we have it before anyone else'. So it was. During mid-afternoon on the day on which the photograph appeared, the marketing director of the ship repair yard telephoned the PR man to thank him for the photograph and said: 'I would have telephoned earlier, but my telephone has been jammed with people wanting to talk about the photograph since I arrived this morning. I have spoken to more customers so far today than I would have during the average month.'

As a bonus the trade media also took the photograph afterwards, so that it then circulated in those parts of the world where the *Daily Telegraph* wouldn't rank high among business reading matter.

Another example of the way in which good and creative use of photography can help lies in the story of two factoring companies, both of which opened offices in Scotland within a few months of one another. The first company, one of the largest, simply issued a press release with a photograph of the local man, billed as the 'Regional Manager for Scotland', which as we noted earlier, would have done little to attract interest or sympathy with the Scottish national media. Absolutely no coverage was obtained. The other company, RoyScot Factors, not only described their new representative in more acceptable terms, but the press release emphasized the growing importance of Glasgow as a financial centre and the likely numbers to be employed in the new office once it was fully established. The Lord Provost was invited to open the new offices and, since the timing of this formal event was inconveniently late in the day for the media, photographs were taken showing the managing director of the company at the opening with the man in charge of the new office. To provide an unusual creative angle, the MD was shown polishing the brass name plate ready for the opening and the newspapers used it. Other angles to the story which also made it more than usually interesting included predictions about the likely future demand from small and medium-sized businesses for factoring services. The result was extensive coverage in the Scottish national press, and in some Scottish regional newspapers with many using the photographs, while there were also radio mentions, often highlighting the need for factoring in a difficult economic climate.

Obviously, photography played only a part in obtaining this coverage, but this is often the case. There are occasions when the photograph will be the story on its own, as with the shipyard and the Chinese characters, but more usually, the photograph will add an extra dimension to the story. Not only does it increase the space given to the story, but as already mentioned, it attracts the eye in the way that a story without a photograph could not do.

COMMISSIONING PHOTOGRAPHY

Despite the importance of photography and the immense use of photographic material in media relations and employee communications, the one person most PR departments and consultancies will seldom have on their staff will be a photographer! This might seem strange, but there are several reasons for this, and for not expecting the PR practitioners to act as photographers themselves in the absence of a true professional on their staff.

Contrary to popular belief, one seldom saves money by having one's own staff photographer, unless the department is so large and the demand for photography so constant, that a photographer can be kept fully employed, but this is rare. A busy company's PR department is likely to find that a staff photographer is unoccupied for four-fifths of the time, and then in demand in two places at once – sometimes planning can resolve such problems, but in many cases the PR function is reacting to events, or attempting to be reactive and proactive at the same time. Another problem with having a staff photographer is that travelling time and travelling costs, which can be considerable given the amount of equipment which photographers often need, eat into any savings.

Specialist photographers

Yet, these are far from being the sole or indeed the most important reasons for not having a photographer on the staff. The more valid reason is simply that photographers are not all alike, but in common with many other professionals, they specialize. Good newspaper photography is often produced by photographers who travel as lightly as possible, and are adept at seeing a news 'angle' or an opportunity, so much so that often newspaper photographers and reporters will work independently of one another, while the pictures desk has its own editor, who will have, in addition to his own photographers, access to agency photographs and to the work of freelancers, appreciating that his own team will not always be in the right place at the right time, and even when they are there, human frailty and the unforeseen might mean that they do not always produce the best photographs. One can sometimes see evidence of news agency or picture agency photography when the photograph accompanying a maor news story is the same in several different newspapers.

Photographers, like artists, have their own style and interests. Premises are treated so much better by architectural photographers than by someone chosen at random, and this is especially so if interior shots, which can create problems with lighting, are required and, in the case of colour photography, with the end result being tinted by a predominant colour in the decorations or furnishings. Other specialized photographers include fashion, travel, aeronautical, aerial, industrial, commercial (or product), medical, wildlife and, of course, portraiture. Apart from differences in location, it is fairly common for a PR function to need one type of photographer on one occasion, and another type of photographer on another.

While being wary of the photographer who claims to be able to handle anything, it is important, for the good of one's budget, if nothing else, to supplement the expensive specialist photographers who can be relied upon to handle the most important work without a hitch, with other cheaper photographers to handle the routine, 'bread and butter' work. A good portrait photograph of the chairman or chief executive for the annual report will require a good portrait photographer, but a simple black and white photograph of a new branch manager for the local newspaper can be safely left to the local general or 'weddings' photographer.

PR involvement

Incidentally, PR involvement in such mundane photography is important, since many managers, asked for a photograph of themselves, often provide something taken in a self-service booth! Such material is completely worthless, and its quality is reflected in the general view that passport photographs seldom bear any visual relationship to the individual concerned! At the other extreme, there was an instance of a regional bank manager who felt that he should always support his customers, and so used one of them who was an extremely expensive professional photographer: he paid £600 for a simple portrait photograph which should have cost no more than a tenth of that sum!

It is not unknown for two or three photographers to be commissioned for a single assignment. For example, some years ago, a Boeing Jetfoil, a type of high speed hydrofoil, was able to travel up the River Thames to the centre of London, passing through Tower Bridge at high tide, while riding at high speed on its foils. There would have been few such opportunities available to the manufacturer or the operator, at any time, and no chance of the Jetfoil going around a second time, if the photographer missed the opportunity. The solution was to use three photographers, two using colour transparency, and the third using monochrome negative film.

Recent amendments to the copyright laws make it imperative that those commissioning photography establish exactly what it is they are buying from the photographer. Because the copyright in a photograph rests with the photographer, he or she will include a copyright element each time they are asked to provide prints. In addition to this traditional practice, today a photographer who has produced a set of colour transparencies for a brochure or a company annual report, can expect a further fee if the work is then used for, say, a magazine article. The answer is to decide exactly what use one will make of the photographs or transparencies, and the period over which that use is likely to be, and stipulate these applications precisely when commissioning the work. It is possible to ask for a blanket transfer of copyright to the customer, but a first class photographer will expect a high fee indeed for this.

The amendments to the copyright laws simply place photographers on the same basis as authors and performing artists, although, oddly enough, journalists and other contributors to newspapers and magazines, still relinquish copyright to the publishers, with a few exceptions.

ORGANIZING PHOTOGRAPHY

Organizing a photographic session is more than simply commissioning a photographer – there are certain important arrangements which the photographer has every right to expect the client to settle, and indeed, which only the client can handle.

The time and place of the photography, the subject which has to be photographed and the object of the exercise are all matters within the control of the client. The degree of involvement will vary, and it is possible to establish a close enough rapport with a photographer, who becomes well known and respected by the client, and also knows and understands the client's business, so that the photographer can be left to handle an assignment on his own. This is a rare situation, and indeed, even those photographer and client relationships which reach this ideal state cannot always function in this way.

The major problem is that the uninitiated, which will mean almost everyone on the client side, simply do not appreciate the problems inherent in good photography. Their view of photography is based on their own use of a camera while on holiday or at a family occasion, or on the work of wedding photographers. They fail to understand that a portrait photograph demands that the photographer portrays his subject in the best possible manner, and that he copes successfully with such difficulties as reflections from the subject's spectacles or off his bald patch, or in the case of colour photography, the phenomenon known as 'red eye', when the flash is reflected by the blood vessels at the back of the eye. That apart, he will be expected by the client, or at least by the client's PR person, to produce formal and informal poses, smiling for good news, and a more serious expression for bad news such as a bad set of annual results! Picture editors do not like photographs in which the subject is staring 'off the page', so there will be a need for left and right facing photographs, and for some facing the camera. Finally, if colour and black and white material are both required, the best results demand that the photographer conducts the whole exercise twice!

This assumes that the visiting photographer can use a room with decent lighting and plain backgrounds, and that the photographer himself has the common sense to check that the end result will not be a print with a metal bar or window frame growing out of the subject's head. These arrangements are necessary since businesspeople seldom visit a photographer in his studio, where suitable backgrounds and lighting would be available.

The whole exercise also requires adequate power points for the photographer, and decent seating for the subject. The photographer will not rely solely on flash, but will augment this with other lighting as well, not least so as to ensure that colour tints do not appear on the end result.

This all takes time, and it is useful for the photographer to be able to visit the scene of the photography in advance, and to be allowed an hour or so to set up his lighting, and perhaps to practise poses with a stand-in subject, so that the time of the subject is kept to the minimum.

Needless to say, the situation is that much worse if a group photograph is needed.

Other photography, such as shots of people working, perhaps inside a factory or an office, can also be difficult, and really require the presence of the PR person to negotiate with management or others involved, since people will be asked to perform certain poses or functions as the photographer attempts to meet his brief, and indeed one cannot pretend that the whole situation will proceed without some difficulty or interruption to work. If a demonstration of a product is being photographed, the product will be put through its paces repeatedly so that eventually, out of the vast collection of material taken, there will be enough useable photographs or transparencies.

Apart from the time element, one cannot use a studio setting for everything, and indeed, studio photography of a product is far more likely with advertising or marketing photography than with PR which, because it is so media-dominated, has to provide good 'action' shots for the newspapers, rather than the sometimes cold and sterile advertising or brochure material.

It is important that the photographer understands why photography is needed, so that he can bring his experience and creativity to bear. If it is for a prestige brochure, he might take a different approach from that required for a magazine, for example. The photography might be simply for record purposes, or it might indeed so affect the way in which the story is handled, that the press officer handling the project might simply issue a photograph and caption rather than bother with a wholly unnecessary press release. This, of course, also means that the photographer must be briefed on the subject, be it a product, new equipment or premises.

One will also have to decide whether the subject will be enhanced by the use of models or by having employees in a work setting. Generally, product photography seems more alive if someone is shown using the product, but, of course, much depends on the product, and such an approach is not possible with an airliner at 35,000 feet, although in such circumstances, exterior air-to-air photography would be complemented by interior shots of the flight deck and passenger cabin, with crew and, when appropriate, passengers.

Good photography takes time, time for the photography itself, and time in preparation, all of which goes some way to explain why using PR people as amateur photographers is not cost-effective, and one is unlikely to find that the results will be as good as those attainable by the professionals!

MAINTAINING A PHOTO LIBRARY

In an ideal world, every PR function or consultancy would have an
experienced, interested and dedicated photo-librarian working for
them. Reality and common sense suggest that such a solution would
be expensive and beyond most budgets, excepting, of course, the
largest organizations. This is unfortunate, since a good photo-
librarian can easily save organizations far more than the usually
modest cost of their salary, but one also has to accept that even
companies, and others, who find photography important, would be
hard put to establish a full-time position. Equally, a lot of damage
can be done to good collections of photographic material by
unsympathetic, or more usually, undisciplined conduct in the
absence of the librarian. When the PR function requires photographs, usually for media use, it needs them quickly.

Essential steps in the management of a photo library, no matter
how big or how small, include:

1. *Storage:* Colour transparencies should be filed in special plastic
   hanging wallets, which enable the transparencies to be viewed,
   and which protect them from dust and dirt. Black and white
   photographs should be filed in hanging files and within acid-
   free wallets to ensure their survival.

2. *Indexing:* Every item needs to indexed and cross-indexed by
   subject, location and date. For example, if one wanted a photo of
   HMS Ark Royal sailing in the Mediterranean during a
   particular year, one would have to index by the name of the
   ship, the Mediterranean and the year, but one would also have
   to say which ship of this name was the subject, since several
   warships (three of them aircraft carriers) have carried this
   name over several centuries, and one might also want an index
   entry under aircraft carriers as well. One would also need to
   indicate the type of photograph: colour transparency, colour
   negative or monochrome. Fortunately, most indexing is simpler
   than this extreme example. Computerization is a distinct
   benefit for this work if material can be cross-indexed two or
   more times. On the other hand, a simple photo library, with
   material filed under subject, such as branches or products, and
   then alphabetically, which would be the case for some
   manufacturers and retailers, could be self-indexing, and
   manual systems will be perfectly adequate.

3. *Captioning:* Every illustration, whether it is a colour transparency or a print, should have a caption, with prints having this pasted, using a suitable non-destructive adhesive, on the back, while transparencies or negatives should be indexed against a caption.

4. *Stock control:* Nothing is more frustrating, and more damaging to the reputation of the PR function, than to find the last (and needless to say, urgently required) photograph of an important subject has been used. No one should take the last one, or even the second or third to last, unless, additional stocks have been re-ordered. Always keep the name, address, fax and telephone numbers of the photographer on file. If the PR function is divided between significant geographical locations, the most important photographs should be stocked in both locations. It is no use a journalist in London demanding a photograph of the chairman or chief executive, or of head office, if that is not held in London. Indeed, large organizations based 'out of town' might do well to have a stock of photographs based at a London office or a consultancy, ready for such an eventuality.

5. *Up-dating:* People age, and buildings, their interiors and equipment change. There should be periodic reviews of the library so that the most important photographs are replaced by more up-to-date illustrations. Whenever a new branch is opened, new vehicles which carry the company's livery ordered, or new equipment of any significance introduced, copies of the photographs, which will probably be taken anyway, should be added to the library.

6. *History:* Organizations develop and even the newest will soon have a history, a past, and records of this will be invaluable in the future. Always have a historical file or section in any photographic library, and have arrangements for suitable material to be transferred, and unsuitable material destroyed as soon as it is no longer current. It is not unknown for journalists, and others, to ask urgently for a current photograph of a branch, vehicle or employee in uniform, and for a historical photograph.

Success in photographic terms, as in anything else in PR, lies in meeting the need immediately. Occasionally an obscure demand will justify a little time in meeting a request, but more often, the request is fairly simple. Every organization should be able to illustrate its activities, and at least the main points in its history, by which one should not only mean significant events or changing chairmen, but changes in the image and the public perception of the organization.

CHECKLIST

- Review your organization's photographic requirements: are any opportunities overlooked?

- Are your existing photographers ideally suited to the type of photography required, to the locations (is too much money wasted in travelling time) and to the budgets?

- Is your photography better or worse than that of your competitors?

- Does PR have its own collection of photographic material ideally suited to editorial requirements?

- Is the photographic collection indexed and up-to-date?

- Are stocks of standard photographs ample for press office needs, relevant and also suitably captioned?

- Do you have the relevant details, including the names of the photographers, telephone numbers and addresses, and the photographers' reference numbers for their work so that additional photographs can be ordered quickly and easily?

9

Supporting Material

The press release or press conference is not always enough in itself, even when supported by a good photograph or colour transparency, or even a background note providing additional information, especially for technical journalists.

Journalists sometimes need more than a simple press release. On occasion, a copy of a brochure or brochures and price lists might be extremely useful to the press, although generally they are not interested in advertising material as such. Often, background material on the organization itself and its achievements will be useful, especially if the organization is not well known to the press, or perhaps not well known enough to a new journalist. In other cases, the press may wish to see and inspect, even sample, a product in some way. The extent to which this is possible varies, as one might expect, since it is impossible to sample a mortgage or a life assurance policy! One would expect few volunteers to sample a major operation even it were to be conducted privately! Journalists might be very welcome to a preview of a new range of fashions, but it would be highly unlikely for anyone to be provided with free samples because of cost and security considerations as leading designers protect their work from their mass production imitators.

Once again, careful thought and preparation is important so that the exercise is neither over- nor under-done, and it is important to avoid providing too many 'free loaders' with free trips to exotic destinations, or the free use of a stylish sports car for a week! While the main media are important, and one can target journalists using *PR Planner*, *PR Targeter* or, even better, one's own well-tried and trusted contacts, the importance of knowing the media and those journalists most likely to be interested in your organization cannot be underestimated. Never overlook the freelance journalists either, since one good freelance journalist is often worth half-a-dozen or more 'staffers', since the freelance is only paid for work which is used, and this has to happen frequently in order for him or her to maintain any reasonable standard of living.

BACKGROUND MATERIAL

In general, background material can be regarded as a whole range of items over and beyond a basic press release, speech, or photograph, including:

- Product literature, such as brochures, technical specifications and price lists.

- Background material on the organization, which can include a potted history, or perhaps a more expensive and glossily produced company history, and annual reports.

- Biographical material on leading individuals within the organization, with good portrait photographs.

Journalists on the general pages of a newspaper writing a story on a major new development will not want to be burdened with brochures and price lists, but will instead expect the press release to provide enough information, including some typical prices and even a price range. In the case of financial products, the cost of a typical mortgage, stating which type of mortgage, would be more useful than a list of mortgages and glossy brochures. If rates have changed, a table showing the cost of four or five typical mortgages would be useful, especially if this is in a form which can be reproduced with acknowledgement given to your organization.

The use of brochures and price lists tends to be more useful to the specialized features writers, who will often file the information so that they can compare products from rival companies from time to time. This means, of course, that once one starts to provide such information, one cannot stop, but must ensure that every journalist who writes regularly on a particular topic is provided with up-dated material as and when it becomes available. Hopefully, they will also contact you to check the information in their reviews before publishing comparisons, but there is the risk that occasionally an out-of-date price list or rate card will be used.

Detailed technical information attached to a press release will often be essential in releasing information on industrial products, including ships and aircraft, to the specialized technical media, but some of the specialized correspondents of the quality press will also appreciate such material.

Background information on the organization, even if it is a charity or pressure group, is especially useful if the media concerned do not know the organization well. This frequently happens if a pressure group launches a new campaign, or if a manufacturer diversifies into a new area of business. Organizations of any kind which move into a new geographical area will also find such material is appreciated by the local media. Inevitably, even well-known companies will find that there are journalists at a press conference or making a factory visit, for example, who are new to the company and to its sector, and again, will need background material. Even if the business, or any other organization, is well-known, it is useful to keep some 'kits' of background information on hand to offer to 'new' or 'strange' journalists.

Media attitudes to receiving copies of the annual report will vary, depending on both whether the annual report is one which contains information about current and recent projects or progress, or whether it is purely a dry financial document. Some journalists will appreciate having the annual report and find even the accounts informative, while others will be baffled by the figures.

Biographical notes and photographs of leading members of an organization are really only necessary if there is a press conference or if the personalities involved are making a speech at a major conference. Offering the biographical notes on the chairman of the board will be a waste of time if the press have arrived to look at a new car or a new home computer.

SAMPLING THE PRODUCT

The popular image of some specialized journalists must be that they spend their lives testing new, and often exotic, motor cars, boats and even aircraft! Obviously such activities must be enjoyable and the author has still to come across a motoring correspondent, for example, who hates his work, still less a yachting journalist or one of that very rare breed of aeronautical journalists who can actually fly and test aircraft. Nevertheless, even enjoyable activities have a serious purpose, and if a journalist is allowed to sample a product, it is for one good reason: the manufacturers, or in some cases the importers or distributors, believe that it will be to their benefit for the product to be so tested, and that the resulting editorial coverage will attract the interest of potential customers. The journalists, and their editors, believe that their readers, or in some cases, viewers, will also be interested.

Product sampling is not the preserve of journalists. The producers and presenters of popular music programmes on radio will often receive advance copies of new recordings, while other producers and presenters may receive review copies of new books, in addition to these being sent to the literary editors of newspapers and magazines.

It does happen that some products will be given editorial coverage without being sampled. In many trade publications, new products, such as new types of bathroom tile or new office desks, will be mentioned, perhaps with a photograph. In those cases in which a reader enquiry service is provided, the reader can ask for literature and perhaps, in the case of the bathroom tile for example, even a free sample. A new type of mortgage or a special feature of a new insurance policy, may also result in free editorial coverage by the personal finance columnists in their regular weekly features.

On the other hand, many household products – new wines, consumer goods of many kinds, and even some of the more portable business products – will have much of their editorial coverage dependent upon a successful sampling of the product by a specialized journalist.

In the case of the new motor car, often journalists will first sample the car at a venue well away from their usual home territory. The whole exercise will be conducted under an embargo, so that the journalists have their story prepared well in advance, ready for the launch date. On such first acquaintanceship with the car, the large number of journalists wishing to test drive examples of the new car will mean that several journalists will share a vehicle for a day or two, and the impressions could be fairly superficial. If this is so, it is usual for a longer test, of a week or so, to be provided later, but not too much later. In the case of cars, the introduction of new versions of the original, perhaps estate car versions of a saloon, or saloon versions of a hatchback, for example, will provide another opportunity for both the manufacturer and the journalist to obtain a further story.

The role of the manufacturer can be taken by the importer or sole distributor in the case of a foreign car, while as we saw earlier local dealers can sometimes obtain a road test in their local newspaper if they can loan the motoring correspondent a demonstration car for a few days.

It is usual to allow a journalist to sample a product on his or her own whenever possible, but one exception to this is, not surprisingly, aircraft, where it is usual for a representative of the manufacturer to be present throughout the test!

Venues

The use of an exotic venue for the press launch of a new product is not always necessary. Car manufacturers like it because they can choose a venue where the local roads will show the vehicle off to the maximum benefit, and of course, it does also reduce the risk of premature leaking of the story. Other manufacturers, of perfumes and other fashion products, look for exotic locations again to show the product off to its best advantage, but also because of the tendency for such products to have something of the the showiness of the fashion world attached to them. A new perfume would not seem nearly so exotic if launched in Blackpool, for example.

The use of exotic venues places additional strains on planning and organizing such launches, and also raises costs. There are other risks. One perfume launch in Egypt caught the world's headlines when the hotel caught fire and a number of leading journalists died. One motor manufacturer took a party of journalists to Portugal in a chartered airliner, fortunately without accident or incident, but of course the cream of the motoring press, and the motoring correspondents of the general press, could have been lost had the worst happened. Perhaps one should temper extravagance with reason, unless, that is, one wishes to undertake a crisis management course first!

PRESS TRIPS AND VISITS

The idea that journalists should be encouraged to sample a product has its parallel in the travel business. Tourist boards and the operators of cruise ships, entertainment complexes and holiday camps, actively seek the attentions of travel writers. Transport operators undertake the same role, but often they have to promote the destination to promote their services. For example, if one is operating car ferries to France, one promotes the ferry service by promoting the destination. The same applies to air services.

Good transport and travel promotion is often a cooperative venture. The cooperation of a transport operator, a tourist board, and perhaps some hotels, can contribute to a successful event. There are journalists who will, in return for a free trip across the English Channel, write a travel story and give the ferry operator or airline a mention, while sometimes a tourist board will approach a transport operator seeking free tickets for a press party in return for an exclusive mention by the press of the operator's services. The exact methods vary, and it is not unknown for transport operators to approach the tourist board in a particular region or country and seek free bed and board for journalists using their shipping or air services.

Of course, resorts are not the only places visited by journalists. There are factories, testing grounds and research institutes which can provide an opportunity for a visit, and often manufacturers will encourage this type of visit because it might provide good editorial coverage, but even if it doesn't, it can still enhance the media's impression of the company and its products, and so improve the quality of future reviews or tests by the specialized correspondents.

The advance preparation of motoring columns and travel articles or programmes contrasts with much of the work of those interested in covering the performing arts. New theatrical productions will often have the press present at a dress rehearsal shortly before the production opens, with the review appearing on the first night or the following day. Press appearances at first nights can still result in reviews in the following morning's newspapers, but much depends on the technology used by the newspaper and the ability to change material between editions. Obviously, for the PR practitioner handling the performing arts, early coverage is often not enough since advance coverage is essential, unless valuable seats are to be left empty at the outset of a new production. This is especially true of many provincial theatre productions, and especially if the only medium is a local weekly newspaper. One solution can be to arrange interviews and background features on the production, while photographs taken at a dummy dress rehearsal or during the play being staged in another town, if the cast hasn't changed, can help. Ideally, staging a dress rehearsal for the local newspaper's own photographer is the best means of attracting coverage, not least because newspapers are most likely to use photographs taken by their own people and, of course, ideally do not like to acknowledge that the play has been shown in another town first.

Not all press trips are fun or, to use a term which is much used, are 'PR jollies'. There are others with a more serious purpose.

Charities inviting journalists to see their work in the field can ask that the media meet their own travel and accommodation costs, and can argue that this is a cost which they cannot provide for fear of diminishing the funds available for their own work.

Who to invite?

In organizing visits by the press to holiday destinations, it can help to improve the resulting features coverage if the press party consists of a mixture of journalists from non-competing publications. Usually the ideal size of a group should be between six and eight journalists, and it can help to improve the atmosphere of the party if spouses are also invited. Journalists from one or two quality newspapers, from a tabloid, from a women's interest magazine, from a provincial press group or two, can provide a well balanced party. Allowing flexibility in the itinerary for journalists to follow their own particular interests, be they shopping, old churches, museums or, even (and it has happened in one notable case) old railways, can also enhance the quality and variety of the coverage. One or two good freelancers will also help to ensure that the trip pays its way in terms of column inches.

By contrast, when launching a new car, one has to ensure that the main newspapers are all included, and if space is limited, a judgement will have to be made over who should be excluded, operating on the basis of who one can most afford not to include or, indeed, who one can risk offending? The risk must be recognized; one European motor manufacturer once upset the British press by letting the German press preview a new car well in advance of the arrangements made for the British. If the vehicle is being introduced into different national markets gradually, then a rolling programme of tests must be arranged, but for those at the end of the queue, some compromise, perhaps a much shortened test, must be provided if national rivalries are to be overcome.

Of course, when organizing any opportunity for a product to be sampled or for a visit or press trip, it is important to ensure that the media concerned can provide the editorial coverage required, either on the news pages or the features pages, and occasionally both. There is no point letting journalists have review copies of books if there is little chance of a review in a newspaper or magazine or an interview with the author on a suitable radio programme. There is no point offering a radio or television interview with the star in a play or an operatic performance if the media concerned do not offer such a facility, or if it is offered to the producer of the wrong programme. Not only will the medium in question be wasted, but even if they did provide a review or an interview, it would be reaching the wrong readers or listeners. If a radio programme, for example, has regular coverage of forthcoming arts events, it will attract a particular kind of listener, but if it is more attuned to the price of fresh produce in the local shops, then it will attract listeners who are more interested in shopping opportunities. On the other hand, it is wrong to subject a busy author to a punishing schedule of radio and television interviews unless one is absolutely certain that all of them will be worthwhile. One should beware of programme producers who are short of material, and if there is likely to be a demand for this type of interview, offer pre-recorded interview tapes as a compromise.

The point about different broadcasting stations and different programmes reaching different audiences can also be applied to newspapers. The *Guardian*, for example, is more concerned with the arts and social issues than with business and financial news, for which, obviously, the *Financial Times* is pre-eminent, while the *Daily Telegraph* and *The Times* try to offer a broader range of editorial fare to their readers. The *Independent* lies somewhere between *The Times* and the *Guardian*. A popular tabloid newspaper is unlikely to be able to offer quite the coverage or depth on many subjects that one might receive from a quality broadsheet, but sometimes a paragraph or two in, for example, the *Daily Mirror*, might be all that one needs. One building society received just this treatment for a new household insurance scheme which offered discounts for people aged 55 years or older, and found that it was swamped with enquiries for the following ten days! Four short paragraphs in the Plymouth *Western Morning News* produced a substantial volume of new business for the local branch of a bank. Quality is as important as quantity, and in this context 'quality' means the impact of the editorial coverage on the organization and not the quality of the publication. One's organization or one's clients might prefer to see a reasonable amount of space in *The Times*, but often less space in a popular newspaper will have more impact.

10

Organizing Features Services

If one looks through the editorial contact pages of the *UK Press Gazette*, one will see that some of the organizations listed offer features services. Editors can telephone and ask for an article on this subject or that, depending on the business of the organization concerned. Why do they do it? What is a features service? How does it, or how can it, work? Is the concept confined to the printed media, or can it work with broadcasting as well?

THE ROLE OF FEATURES

The role of features has already been touched upon, and the value of features in providing additional background coverage, has been outlined. The importance of specialized features in providing an opening for smaller developments in personal finance or other consumer interests, has already been emphasized. Nevertheless, a features service is more proactive than this. In many cases, features are prepared by the staff journalists working for a newspaper or magazine, or by well-respected freelance journalists, because they feel that a major development requires more explanation. The view is that the reader will expect to know more, and in effect have a briefing on the impact of a major development. In regular features on domestic matters, travel, motoring or personal finance, the editor of that particular section of a newspaper pulls together recent product developments so that the reader can quickly up-date himself or herself on what is available. Good or innovative products will often be highlighted and recommended in some way; less worthy products will simply be mentioned, or if too mundane, will not be covered at all. Poor products can expect criticism, and the providers of the product might hope that it escapes editorial notice – which is not always possible if a dissatisfied customer complains, for example.

Providing a features service

In providing a features service, the public relations functions of various organizations are taking the initiative and writing their own material.

The most important aspect of this development is that one must be fully aware of what a features service can and can't do. A features service will *not* propel your products or the opinions of your chief executive straight onto the front page of the leading newspapers! For a start, such newspapers reserve the front page for news, not features. Secondly, such newspapers either have their own journalists writing their material, or commission freelance features writers to do it for them.

The role of a features service is to provide material for those publications which are so under-resourced that they cannot provide all of the necessary editorial material themselves. This usually means trade and business publications, as well as many local newspapers. A substantial number of provincial evening newspapers and some provincial regional morning newspapers will also accept this kind of material.

The quality of the newspaper will often determine what can, and equally what cannot, be published. Most local freesheets will be delighted to take a features service as 'advertorial', that is, as part of an editorial and advertising package. Nevertheless, the best features services are those which are sufficiently good that newspapers will be happy to run them without having advertising as an inducement. The low editorial content of the worst freesheets will sometimes mean that these will only take features supported by advertising.

The better quality freesheets, many provincial evening and some provincial morning newspapers, as well as the trade and business press, will often be prepared to consider free publication of articles of the desired quality. The basic rules are:

- Offer the article to the features editor or the editor (trade, business and local newspapers seldom have a features editor) with a short covering letter, briefly describing the content.

- If a series of features is being offered, send one or two samples, again with a brief covering letter, and of course mention just how many features will be included and how frequently these can be provided.

- Ensure that the features are of a length suitable for publication in the newspaper in question. One should enquire if there should be any doubt over the required length. Trade and business publications will vary widely in their expectations, but newspapers will seldom want more than 1200–1500 words, and most will want much less than this. Local newspapers might want just 300-500 words, the better newspapers might accept 600 words, and a few will take 800–1000 words. Always write to length, since this reduces the risk of the editor making cuts which might lose what you consider to be important, or the even greater risk of a busy editor or chief sub editor not bothering, and simply dropping the article altogether!

- Good features must appear to be impartial, so don't keep mentioning your organization in the feature, and never knock competitors unless, of course, you have been asked for a highly partisan piece by an editor attempting to stimulate controversy.

- Ideally, restrict the editorial mention to the job title of the author of the article (whether or not he or she really is the author). It is usually a good idea in the local and regional press to ensure that it is your local manager who is given as the author, building in the reference to the author and the organization in the by-line so that it becomes, for example, 'by John Smith, York Manager, Brown's Insurance Services' rather than some distant head office personality. This provides the local connection which is so much more useful both to your organization and to the newspaper.

- Features which do not mention the organization's name or products in the main copy are more credible than those which consistently appear to promote them.

- Look for subjects which enable your organization to appear as interested and concerned providers of impartial advice in your organization's field.

- Make the features more attractive to editors by promising semi-exclusivity, which means that not only will competing publications not be offered the articles once accepted, but those in adjoining circulation areas will also be excluded. The last thing the editor of a newspaper wants is for people to believe that he is taking a cheap way out in filling editorial space. If the article or articles should be accepted by the *Bristol Evening Post*, for argument's sake, do not offer the same material to the *Bath & West Evening Chronicle*, or to the Gloucester, Cheltenham or Exeter evening newspapers. Editors do not mind running the same news story, especially if they all have the story at the same time, but features are different.

• Finally, never let an editor down by failing to provide all of the articles promised. Wise editors will have all of the articles in their possession before starting to publish, but sometimes this is not possible. Always up-date articles if they are overtaken by developments between writing and publication. If a regular article is promised, always give the editor good advance warning before ending the arrangement, say, a month for weekly newspapers.

BROADCAST FEATURES

The introduction of sponsorship of radio and television programmes in the United Kingdom has opened up a new possibility for promoting companies or brands, but this practice should not be confused with a features service. The current rules are that sponsors should not influence programme-making, and should not be in the same business as the programme's subject. This means, for example, that it is fine for a credit card company to sponsor a holiday programme on television, but it would be wrong for an airline, a tour operator or a tourist board to do so. The rules are sensible – if the integrity of programme-makers is diminished, the value of the programme and the importance of a favourable mention will be lost forever. At the same time, a credit card company can benefit directly from being associated with a holiday programme, or indeed, any programme which encourages the viewer to commit himself or herself to major expenditure.

By broadcast features, we mean something rather different from programme sponsorship, or indeed, from the video news releases mentioned in Chapter 5. In common with a features service, broadcast features are used by local radio stations to overcome the limitations of their programme budgets. Short radio tapes, usually taking an interview format, are produced on behalf of companies and other organizations by one of a small number of specialist producers. It is usual for the producer to offer a package which includes help in preparing an interview with someone from the organization commissioning the tape, the services of a professional interviewer, and distribution to a set number, say 20 or so, local radio stations. The producer will offer advice on those radio stations most likely to accept such material, usually after discussing with the commissioning organization those parts of the country which need to be targeted.

Broadcast features are not normally kept on file and issued whenever a radio station asks for one. Radio stations who want an interview will organize it themselves rather than telephone expecting to have a tape sent to them. The broadcast feature or interview issued on behalf of a company is sent out usually on a speculative basis, but in common with the video news release, it should be dealing with a topic of current interest.

Problems and tips

The major problem in using such a service is that many radio presenters will introduce the tape, using the cue sheet provided by the production company, but often omitting such vital elements as the name of the organization. Take, for example, the presenter of a holiday programme who uses the following introduction:

> 'Now that the holiday season is with us, many of you will be planning to take your car abroad. Janet Smith speaks to John Brown about some of the new ferry services now available.'

All very well, but what John Brown's company actually wanted was:

> 'Now that the holiday season is with us, many of you will be planning to take your car abroad. Janet Smith speaks to John Brown of Biscay Ferries about some of the new ferry services now available.'

The whole point is that the mention of the company name is necessary and is on a par with the by-line in the features service. Without it, much of the benefit is lost unless, of course, our fictional example, Biscay Ferries, were to be the sole operator on a particular route, and so could still benefit from a mention of the new service. The solution is to do precisely what one should try to avoid doing with a newspaper feature, and mention one's organization once during the interview, and do it in the middle of an answer in such a manner that it seems natural, and cannot easily be edited out of the interview.

Many people find radio interviews difficult, but the producer of the tape and the interviewer will be working for your organization and should be ready to help get it right. The most important points are:

- Be clear in advance why you wish to commission a tape, and go over what you have to say. A strong message, of interest and relevance will be used: one which is pure waffle, boring or on a subject so obscure that the average radio listener will not be interested, will be a waste of time, effort and money.

- Have a loose script available, but attempt to keep the interview as free and as natural as possible. Too tight a list of questions makes it difficult for the interviewer to ask supplementaries and develop the interview in the way that a radio station interviewer would do.

- Don't script your answers, but answer in your own words.

- Don't be afraid of trying it again if the interview doesn't work the first time round, but never let this be a substitute for preparation, since many interviewees tend to perform best the first time round, and the standard often falls away after the second or third attempt, and few people produce a decent interview on the sixth or seventh attempt. The producer can edit the best questions and answers from the different takes, to produce a more polished tape for issue, but this sometimes lacks the flow of a good interview.

- Keep the interview short: five minutes on radio is a long time!

- Finally, in addition to accepting the production company's feedback on the number of radio stations using the tape, also make sure that the broadcast monitoring companies are on the look-out for mentions of your organization so that transcripts can be ordered. This is the only way of being sure whether or not the tape has been worthwhile. In cost-benefit terms, half-a-dozen stations broadcasting the interview will be more cost-effective than radio advertising, while a dozen uses can be a great success, providing, of course, that your organization's name or its products have been mentioned.

11

Centralize or Decentralize?

Organizations and their structures vary. It is foolish to believe that there is a standard model which every business, charity or pressure group can use since size, geographical spread, the nature of the activity being undertaken, and the ownership structure can all influence the way in which an organization operates. The corporate culture is also important. Even in the same industry, structures will vary; the definition of a successful structure is that it is the one which works for the organization concerned, while the wrong structure is the one which doesn't work. Whether the organization is heavily centralized or decentralized depends more on management philosophy, the industrial situation and the individual company, as well as the geographical spread and the variety of products produced. There is a view that decentralized structures are more efficient since they give subsidiary or divisional management greater freedom and encourage initiative, but while this is still the fashionable view, there can be problems, waste and duplication, and even confusion, with this approach. Some companies which officially decentralize do so within such tight guidelines that there is less management opportunity than might appear to be the case to an outsider. Others are conglomerates which buy and sell subsidiaries as market conditions dictate, and do not look beyond the bottom line of the subsidiaries, still less desire a uniform corporate culture.

CENTRALIZED OR DECENTRALIZED
PUBLIC RELATIONS

Public relations, including media relations, has little option other than to follow the pattern of the organization generally, but there are certain aspects of PR which occasionally suggest special treatment. There is also a difference between corporate and financial media relations on the one hand, and media relations in support of marketing objectives on the other. The former may be compared with the board functions or with the work of the internal audit or accountancy departments, while the latter is linked to the individual sales and marketing functions of the different divisions or subsidiaries within the overall business.

It is common for conglomerates to have widely disparate subsidiaries, often widely spread geographically, and PR, including media relations, is left to the individual subsidiaries for the most part. The exception to this is that head office has control of all aspects of media relations as applied to the performance of the conglomerate as a whole, to its strategy and, of course, company acquisitions or disposals. The extent to which the head office media relations function will become involved with the work of subsidiaries will depend on the prevailing culture. If the subsidiaries are linked to the parent by a common corporate identity, suggesting a longer-term and more permanent relationship than in those companies where the parent acts purely as a holding company or investment vehicle, the need for coordination and closer links is stronger because everything the subsidiaries do reflects on the parent. Indeed, the use of such an endorsed corporate identity implies that the parent wishes to show the world just how diverse its business is. Often, such companies are not as diverse in their activities as a true conglomerate, and the businesses have a common link with diversification being within a sector or industry, such as transport, defence equipment, food, chemicals or financial services. In other conglomerates there may be few business links between subsidiaries and little cohesion. This has its problems, as the PR director of one such widely diversified group once put it to the author: 'I hate to think what might be happening in some of the subsidiaries, and its implications for us if the media and the politicians were to discover something nasty.'

Of course, well diversified companies keep sales and marketing, as well as PR, at divisional or subsidiary level.

On the other hand, a strongly integrated group with just one or two core businesses will want the consistency of a centralized PR function, albeit sometimes with people on detachment at various locations, especially if the geographical spread is wide. Good examples of this approach are found in the major airlines, and other large international organizations. Even big organizations with a purely national business will sometimes have PR people in different centres, but with reporting lines to the head office, so that the head office is aware of local or regional developments. Oil companies also take this approach. If the culture of the organization is to encourage local or regional management to take initiatives, then PR will follow the same pattern; a good example of this is British Rail. Government departments each have their own media relations function, and indeed the Ministry of Defence maintains separate teams for the three armed services as well as having media relations people in major overseas commands.

Problems of coordination

An absence of coordination does give rise to problems, and unfortunately the ability of general management to appreciate these difficulties usually only occurs once it is too late. Coordination does not simply mean clipping the wings of those employed in subsidiaries, but being aware of local initiatives. It is true that locally-based or divisionalized media relations improves the chances of effectively targeting media relations, and makes this role far easier than it otherwise would be. On the other hand, sometimes efforts are duplicated, and unnecessary costs arise. The media can also be confused through the absence of a single, well-managed and coordinated press office. Many years ago, the author once had to speak to three or four different press offices at what was then Hawker Siddeley Aviation, simply to write a story for the *Sunday Telegraph* on the progress of the company's products. No one likes being pushed from one person to another, or having to make several telephone calls when only one should do. It is also often the case that a diversified media relations function is such that no one press office is adequately staffed, and the result is a succession of 'one man bands' with all that this implies for a breakdown in service during absences for leave, sickness or training.

Some solutions

So, what can PR, and especially media relations, do about this? Office politics and human nature combine to ensure that any attempt to impose a central solution will lead to resistance from subsidiary or divisional management, especially when these have been set performance targets. Sometimes the problem lies in the calibre of subsidiary management, who may be frustrated by under-investment or who simply feel that their problems are misunderstood by head office or the parent company, or alternatively might be failed entrepreneurs blaming their own shortcomings on others. Offer local autonomy and other problems arise. One also has to take into account that a subsidiary or a division might be highly active on product development and need substantial media relations help at one time, then might have a quiet period. One solution can be to have a centralized PR function with the capability of seconding experienced staff to individual companies, divisions or locations for a period so that they are close to the management team whom they are supporting, gaining in experience, and yet available to provide additional support elsewhere. The one note of caution with this approach is that the individuals concerned must have sufficient experience to have credibility with the management team they are assigned to, and to show the centralized PR function in a favourable light.

Another solution is to have a strong central staff, but to top up with judicious use of good PR consultancies as and when the need arises. It is no bad thing to keep a short list of good consultancies so that these can be appointed as and when an assignment occurs. It helps to maintain adequate control and to ensure that the service is what one expects if one buys consultancy services from a 'menu' rather than committing one's PR function or a subsidiary to the wholesale appointment of a consultancy.

A difficulty which sometimes arises is whether or not a company located well away from London, for example, needs a local presence there. Some banks and building societies like to have a media relations presence in London rather than in the city in which they have a head office, while others divide the media relations function between their home town and London. The answer lies in just how much senior management is concentrated in London, and how much is located away from the main UK media in the capital. Modern communications mean that the media are instantly accessible from almost anywhere in the British Isles, and it is the management interface which should determine the presence of the media relations specialist.

In short, whenever possible, flexibility is enhanced by keeping the media relations function in as few locations as possible. This approach also reduces costs and improves productivity, and ensures good exchange of information and communication within the PR function as a whole. One must always be prepared to conduct a careful analysis of the problems. Recognizing that media relations effort and effect cannot always be in proportion to one another – something which is often overlooked. Those who shout longest and loudest at the media usually find that resistance sets in, while a succession of good stories and the availability of management personalities for interview can give true success with just a little effort, and considerable skill.

12

The Importance of Careful Planning

Planning is an aspect of media relations which also has an impact on targeting. Unfortunately, the ability of a good press office to draft, clear and release a statement to the media within a very short time leads many managers, including those in marketing, to assume that media relations is an activity capable of producing a quick result. True, it is capable of doing so, but only when the item is sufficiently newsworthy as to ensure attention from the media. This type of media relations is fine for the announcement of a major contract, even for bad news, or to counter and correct criticism, but there is little in media relations which is not handled better and produces a better result than some advance preparation.

DEADLINES

There are also those stories which can be misunderstood if released at the wrong time. Financial journalists are extremely sceptical about any story which a company releases after the stock markets have closed on a Friday, simply because it is so difficult for them to get their stories researched and written in time, and because stock market reaction cannot be gauged. Not only do many business pages have an earlier deadline than the general news pages, but the *Financial Times* has an earlier deadline than most newspapers. Journalists writing on business and finance, and especially those concerned with the stock markets, are at their busiest in the late afternoon and early evening.

Earlier, we saw also the importance of timing and working well in advance to ensure coverage in many women's magazines. There is a need to ensure that adequate timing and scheduling is present whenever a new product or a major development, such as a new factory or office, is planned.

If a product is to be regarded as 'news', the media must not be aware of its existence from any other source. This means, for example, that it is imperative when planning a launch to ensure that the information is made available to the media in advance of any advertising, since journalists are there to provide news, not history, and do not like being pipped at the post by advertising. This might sound simple in practice, but it does mean keeping in mind deadlines for those publications which one has targeted, remembering also that advertising deadlines are sometimes far less exacting than those for editorial. This is especially important when the product is one which has to be featured on a particular page or section of a national newspaper, such as a new car or a new financial product, since these special sections are often prepared well in advance, and appear on a particular day of the week. If the journalists have to research the story or sample the product, then timing becomes even more difficult, and one will have to ensure that the media are happy to cooperate with an embargo so that the story does not leak out prematurely.

PLANNING AND COORDINATION

There is in fact a simple three step checklist to bear in mind when launching a new product or service:

- Remember the need to programme PR and advertising so that the news value of the product is not undermined by a premature burst of advertising.

- Ensure that there is adequate pre-launch publicity for dealers or agents so that they are not caught unawares by customer demand for the new product.

- Identify the important media and schedule the release of information so that vital weekly and monthly publications are not at a disadvantage, otherwise these will scale down their coverage if they feel they are lagging too far behind the dailies.

In targeting the market, it is important to bear in mind where the organization is based, if it has its own retail network, as happens with banks and building societies, and where these are located. Simply by using a word processor, press releases can be localized and targeted at newspapers with a branch of the organization in their circulation area. This not only helps to ensure local and regional coverage, reaching still more of the potential market, but also helps to remind would-be customers of your organization's presence in their area. It can also have a beneficial effect on staff morale as well, and not least that of the branch manager, who feels that head office is doing something to help him improve the volume of business handled by his branch.

The same rules apply regardless of the market. For example, the basics of business-to-business media relations in many ways differ little from those for consumer business; it is the choice of techniques which differ, and the pace of work. The same three point plan should be borne in mind.

Exhibitions and conferences gain greater force for business-to-business activity than for consumer work, and the emphasis is, as a rule, more heavily on specialized publications than on the general media. It is important not to overlook regional and local business publications, nevertheless, and to take a different approach to sponsorship, thinking in terms of hospitality as well as entertainment, audience appeal and name awareness.

Of course, it is tempting to sit back and feel that little more can be done following a successful launch, except to ensure that coverage is not lost in the regular features. To take this line is to miss further opportunities. After all, if the product has been a success, why not tell everyone about it. This doesn't mean simply pushing out a press release saying, for instance, that 'the new Sproggs Wunderkar has been a tremendous success', but instead it will be important to say why it has been such a success, quantifying the success. If sales have reached a record, or if market share has increased, or whatever, then say so. As mentioned earlier, in some types of business, there are convenient milestones which can be celebrated, and apart from the millionth passenger, these can include anniversaries for products which have been successful. In the UK, for example, the Rover Group introduced a special development of the MGB sports car to celebrate the thirtieth anniversary of the introduction of the car. Some managements detest talking about success since it means that they will also be expected to talk about a perceived failure, but they might have to do so anyway, so why ignore the good stories when they come to hand? A management able and willing to discuss the bad as well as the good will have enhanced credibility the next time it has a success to proclaim.

CHECKLIST

- Advance preparation is as important for public relations as it is for advertising. Discuss plans for the product with the marketing people at an early stage, and if possible include the production and distribution people, in case unknown factors come to light and your role as a communicator enables you to assist in solving a potential problem.

- Make PR techniques available for internal communication and communication with intermediate external audiences such as dealers or distributors, including newsletters and video when suitable.

- Ensure that you fully understand the product, its benefits, the market, and the strengths and weaknesses of competitive products.

- Identify the main markets and the way in which the product will reach these, through dealers or agents, directly, or whatever.

- Ensure that different types of media are used during the launch period, reaching dealers first, then end users, while making the most of periodicals and regional or local publications.

- Be aware of events which might help the product, and of seasonal demands or opportunities, since these might also influence the launch timetable.

- Use a different, but always appropriate approach, for different markets.

- Look for post-launch opportunities to keep information flowing, including information which will quantify the success of the product.

- Don't forget the dealers or agents after the launch; they will be just as interested in hearing about progress. The business-to-business market is one of the largest in the UK, but it will vary in importance between industries. Companies extracting raw materials are at the start of the chain, and will be less dependent upon other suppliers than will the motor industry, for example, where most manufacturers are, in reality, assemblers of bought-in components.

13

Assessing the Results

As mentioned at the beginning of this book, many people in general management, and sometimes those in marketing and advertising as well, will declare that it is difficult to quantify the benefits of public relations. PR is sometimes described as being 'intangible', and, of course, 'difficult to target', although as we have seen this is nonsense. The cynics might suggest that these misconceptions suit some members of the public relations profession very well, and that they work hard at fostering them!

It is important that public relations is quantified in the same way as any other business activity. Clients and employers must be clear about the benefits of public relations activity, and that must include media relations, as well as being aware of the dangers of not using PR. Public relations, and especially media relations, is meant to be cost-effective, and should never depend simply on being inexpensive. The two criteria, cost and effectiveness are in effect an equation, and must be viewed as such; the emphasis should not be on either costs or effectiveness alone.

There will be a number of ways in which you can apply the measures outlined in this book, and you will find that some of the benefits are not only tangible, but will be available to you and your employer or client at a fairly early stage. Ideally, you will have the benefit of research which shows the position at the outset, so that future progress can be set against this base, but even if you do not have this, progress should be assessed at regular intervals so that any problems can be identified and, hopefully, improvements can be tracked. Growth in the volume of press cuttings and in media interest will follow more careful targeting, but this will not be a one-off improvement, and the progress should gather momentum over a lengthy period. Media relations is, after all, all the better for being part of a longer-term strategic programme rather than a series of ad hoc exercises.

Public relations activity can be assessed and quantified in a number of ways, some of them scientific, while others are perhaps less so. The four principle means of assessing just how effective a public relations campaign has been are research, measurement of press and broadcast coverage, a communications audit or, of course, simply achieving a given result. Each of these methods has its strengths and weaknesses, and sometimes one will need to consider more than one method.

RESEARCH

Research can cover a multitude of sins, since it can often reflect the bias and prejudices of the commissioner. Good objective research needs to be conducted externally, by specialists who appreciate that the phrasing of questions can, if one is not careful, influence the answer. Ideally, if one is measuring the effectiveness of a particular campaign, one should commission research on the target audience before the campaign starts, and then repeat the exercise after it has finished. Only in this way can effectiveness be measured on a campaign basis.

Naturally, many PR people are not engaged in specific campaigns, but are maintaining a continuous programme of communications, and in such a context, 'before and after' research has little to offer. Nevertheless, regular research projects can provide a basis for measuring activity and highlight problems in a PR programme before they become too serious.

Types of research

But how does one commission research, and with whom is it conducted? In fact such decisions are entirely at the discretion of those commissioning the research. There are two main types of research: qualitative and quantitative.

Qualitative research is based on interviews and identifies specific responses or reactions, and may even attribute these to individuals. It follows that to be manageable, such research has to be confined to a limited audience, such as those investment analysts interested in a particular sector of industry, or politicians interested in a particular topic, for example. In some cases, the research will feature the use of groups or panels, and may be conducted by a psychologist. This technique is often used when new products or new advertising campaigns are being evaluated.

Quantitative research poses questions to a larger number of people, but seldom looks for more than a 'yes' or 'no' answer. The best examples of such research are the regular opinion polls conducted to assess the electoral preferences of the population, in which usually a thousand or so people are asked for their political allegiance and whether or not certain politicians are good or bad at their particular jobs. In industry, such research is often conducted into product preferences.

Using outside researchers

It is open to anyone or any organization to identify a research company and ask them to prepare proposals for conducting research into a particular topic. The researchers will need to have a brief so that they can formulate a draft questionnaire and also estimate the likely costs and the timescale. Experienced research-ers will be able to advise on suitable times of the year, the month, the week, or even the day, for conducting research so that one can catch the ideal audience. In many industries, the major research companies will have regular research programmes of their own, so that anyone interested in the sector can subscribe to such research. The advantage of this is that it is much cheaper than going it alone, and often one is able to compare one's own organization with its rivals more easily. Drawbacks include being unable to exert much influence over the questions and the audience among whom the research is being conducted. It is often not possible to use the results in publicity since they are subject to copyright and belong to the research company. Nevertheless, on balance, if such omnibus research projects are available, subscribing to them is an inexpensive way of obtaining information, and provides a starting point from which one can plan other specific commissioned research – in short, ignoring such omnibus research could put one in the position of reinventing the wheel, at great cost!

There are also regular research programmes which cover a variety of industries. Good examples of these include those conducted by MORI into the perceptions of business and finance journalists on the one hand, and personal finance journalists on the other. Such research looks at the attitudes of these audiences towards specific companies contributing to the research, to their management, their products, and not least, their media relations. The weakness of some of the MORI research is that it does not always cover the right journalists and, in the case of banking, for example, many of the business and financial journalists interviewed will not be regular specialist contacts in the field. Such research programmes are often more likely to be qualitative than quantitative. Sometimes, industries or trade associations will combine to commission research.

The time taken for qualitative research interviews means that often it is useful, and even necessary, to offer a financial or other inducement to those being interviewed by the researchers. This raises ethical questions, so often those being interviewed are offered the opportunity of asking the research company to make a donation to a charity of their choice, but the provision of bottles of alcoholic drink, gift vouchers or some suitable gift are not unknown, and so too are cases in which the donation and a gift voucher are both provided! Contrary to popular belief, journalists do not necessarily opt for the alcoholic drink. One survey of 20 journalists offered as an inducement for their help the full choice of drink vouchers, book tokens, theatre vouchers and charitable donations, and most opted for book tokens, with drink being well down the list of preferences!

Research using small groups of people or panels can be useful, especially in tracking trends, but it can be difficult to organize and even more difficult to retain the interest and involvement of those involved. The problem also arises that such work, often used to validate marketing campaigns and television advertising in particular, can soon deteriorate into providing the results which the panel members believe the commissioner wants.

It is never good enough to conduct research by simply sending a questionnaire, since the likely response will be patchy, and perhaps mainly confined to those who are critical of whatever is being provided.

COMMUNICATIONS AUDIT

The communications audit is the classic means of assessing media relations and it is true that such an audit can be extremely useful in assessing whether or not PR is achieving its objectives. Ideally, such an audit should be conducted whenever there is a significant change in the control of the PR function to provide the new departmental head with an assessment of the current position and the strengths and weaknesses of the PR function. It can also be useful if there is a change of consultancy. An annual communications audit is probably too much, especially if one subscribes to annual omnibus research activity of media opinion, but such an audit every three years or so can be valuable and should be easily justified.

The term communications audit might seem rather grandiose, but it is one which can be justified. Just as one will have a financial audit of the organization, and some will have a safety audit to see if their safety procedures are as good as they ought to be, the same measure can be justified for public relations. After all, media relations is not a corporate luxury or a question of prestige, but instead a necessity, a vital element in the management of the organization, a tool in every sense of the word.

There are two questions to set oneself:

1. What are the target audiences, and have these changed recently?

2. Have the media changed, or have there been changes among the journalists involved?

A communications audit does not have to look solely at a particular aspect of the overall PR programme, and neither, on the other hand, does it have to be devoted to a single aspect of PR, such as media relations. There is much to be said for a wide-ranging audit of the way in which internal and external audiences view the organisation, finding out basically just how perceptions mirror the truth. It might be, and indeed it often does happen, that such audits guide the management of an organisation by showing them how others see them, highlighting areas of weakness and of strength. An open mind is important.

Often, a new head of public relations will conduct a communications audit of his own. This can be either qualitative research, in which discussions are held with a limited number of people, or quantitative research, in which a larger number of people are polled, either being interviewed by a researcher with a list of questions, or being asked to complete a questionnaire, with the results produced in a tabulated form.

It is important to appreciate that, even though we are primarily concerned with media relations, a thorough communications audit will often embrace interviews with members of the management team as well as with specific journalists identified as being of importance to the organization.

The best communications audits need to use an external consultant, which may be a major opinion research company or a PR consultant.

Auditing method

The steps in conducting a communications audit are as follows:

1. Identify the scope of the audit – will it be group-wide or something less than this? What communications will be involved?

2. Prepare a brief outlining the background of the organization and its media relations, looking at the environment and taking into account industry changes and, if necessary, changes likely to affect your organization.

3. Identify a short list of possible consultants.

4. Offer the brief to the consultants and discuss the communications audit and the way in which it is to be conducted with them. Also ask for costs. The brief will be further refined and developed during the discussions.

5. Agree the questions to be asked and any competitors with whom your media relations should be compared.

6. Appoint consultants and inform those who might be interviewed on the internal list, insisting that every assistance is to be given. Journalists being interviewed need not be advised in advance, and indeed should not, so that the consultants can conceal the identity of the commissioning organization until after the interviews are completed, to ensure that responses from the journalists are completely objective.

7. The consultants will collate, analyze and present their findings. They may also make recommendations.

If your media relations are normally handled by a PR consultancy, it is best if the audit is conducted by a third party. On the other hand, a new internal communications consultancy might wish to include an audit in its first year's work so that it can plan ahead more effectively, and such a professional approach is to be encouraged.

MONITORING PRESS AND BROADCAST COVERAGE

In most public relations functions, the prime requirement is to obtain a 'good press', although increasingly, this also means good broadcast coverage as well. The obvious means of assessing whether or not media coverage is satisfactory is to ensure that a good press cuttings agency is retained, and by also making use of the services of a company able to monitor broadcasts, providing transcripts whenever the organization is mentioned, and even providing video tapes of television coverage. In fact, no press cuttings agency is better than 70 per cent effective, for the understandable reason that references will be missed sometimes. Since some are better in dealing with one type of publication than another, sometimes it is worth using two agencies. In the case of broadcast monitoring services, some are faster than others, but the slower ones are usually larger and able to provide complete nationwide coverage of local radio and regional television as well as national broadcasts.

It is impossible to scan every newspaper or magazine oneself, and it would be expensive to buy them all, although, of course, most PR functions take the main national and the relevant regional newspapers, as well as those magazines relevant to their industry, or that of their clients. The more often one is mentioned in the media, the more likely it is that the press cuttings agencies and broadcast monitors will recall that one's organization is a client. It is also possible to specify from both types of agency any mention of a rival or of a company which might be the subject of an acquisition.

Cuttings agencies and broadcast monitors work in different ways, and charge differently as well. Cuttings agencies automatically cut, despatch and charge for everything they find, while the broadcast monitors offer a transcript or tape to the client, when relevant, so that there is an opportunity to refuse it, before transcribing and despatching. The difference is simply one of cost, since cuttings are relatively inexpensive, while transcripts and tapes are far more costly. Incidentally, while individual cuttings might cost as much as, or more than, the newspaper from which they have been cut, this is still less expensive than buying everything!

The means of assessing the value of this service are as follows:

1. Measure the number of cuttings and the relevance of the newspapers. The same can be done with broadcast mentions.

2. Measure the length of each cutting, or transcript, so that this can be translated into column inches, and minutes or hours of air time.

3. One can, if necessary, assign a value to the coverage obtained by relating the space or time to advertising rates. Nevertheless, this is only a rough guide because it often cannot provide a cost which reflects the position on the page or the different value of different pages in advertising rate terms, and, most important of all, cannot account for the fact that editorial is read or listened to when advertising might be ignored! In the UK, of course, the BBC does not carry advertising, so any rate comparison becomes of doubtful value. Nevertheless, such a comparison, while time-consuming, is often highly influential with management.

4. Assess whether the coverage is favourable or unfavourable to the organization and its objectives.

PUBLIC RELATIONS BY RESULTS

There are occasions when public relations can be judged fairly on the results of a particular campaign. If the battle is won to influence opinion, success is obvious to all. Such activities are not confined to pressure groups, but can be applied equally well in business. For example, when Direct Line Insurance decided to tackle the charges levied by building societies on those of their borrowers who would not insure their homes through the society, not only did they receive widespread media coverage, but also attracted the support of consumer groups. One doesn't wait for such groups to take notice, one has to lobby them as effectively as one lobbies politicians.

Most PR practitioners should be able to recall a few instances when a specific piece of work has resulted in an easily quantifiable result. The few lines in a newspaper which resulted in a flood of enquiries, perhaps even business, for a product which wasn't even being advertised, for example.

In practice, most PR campaigns can be assessed by the level of support which the organization receives. In some cases this support can be measured by an upswing in business, while for charities an upturn in donations achieves the same end. It can be possible for companies to launch a new product without advertising, simply using good media relations allied to a strong and newsworthy story.

Some trade magazines have reader response cards for editorial as well as advertising, and this does provide a measure of success, at least as far as generation of enquiries is concerned. Judging whether such enquiries are turned into sales is more time-consuming, and the decision on whether or not to do this, and in fact the measurement of success, would belong to the sales and marketing function. When such cards are included, it is not unusual for editorial to generate two or three times the interest created by advertising.

Ideal PR activities for response measurement include new product launches, charitable appeals, and lobbying campaigns, usually those by trade associations to force governments to take, or even not to take, a certain course of action.

Appendix: 21 Points for Targeting and Managing News and Features

It is no bad thing to reduce the essential elements in news management to a number of pointers, a checklist of things to do, or at least watch for, and a few things which should be avoided. Here are 21 points to remember.

1. Be aware of the likely news possibilities emanating from your organization or from your client – those items which are bad news as well as those which are good – so that you are prepared and can handle the news in the best manner.

2. Keep the media contact lists up-to-date, and be aware of who the best contacts will be for a particular story. In addition, ensure that the section editor, be it the news editor, city editor, or sports editor, also receives the story in case your usual contact or the main specialist is absent for any reason.

3. Angle the story for different markets, whether differentiated by interests, age, sex, geography, etc.

4. Bear in mind the different deadlines and publication dates for newspapers and periodicals, especially if one also needs to receive coverage in a major trade or professional publication to support consumer interest.

5. If the story is sufficiently important, call a press conference or press briefing. This has two advantages, it brings senior management and the media into contact, and ensures consistency in dealing with media questions. On the other hand, if a venue is inconvenient, the media might not appear, and if the story is lightweight, their first visit might be their last!

6. Always be aware of seasonal opportunities for products or services, and the regular specialist sections or pages in many general newspapers, including motoring, travel, gardening, home improvement or other features, and, of course, not forgetting special pre-Christmas or spring features. Such special items are often prepared well in advance, however, with popular women's interest magazines finalizing their Christmas features in August.

7. Always be ready to capitalize on, or react to, any events or circumstances which might offer an opportunity for a response. Statements on policy by politicians, or such events as the Budget, the release of trade figures or other official statistics, can all provide opportunities for comment, but sometimes, in addition, the media might expect a reaction. There are advantages in being seen as a good source of comment and opinion, providing that this is handled sensibly, otherwise it can become a trap!

8. If your organization has particular and relevant experience or research which will be of media interest, use it to maintain the relationship with the media at times when other stories are few and far between. Of course, there must be an obvious public, and therefore media, interest in the subject.

9. If a photograph will help to promote the product, or if the media might expect a photograph to accompany a story, ensure that such material is available. When issuing press releases with photographs, most publications will expect monochrome, that is black and white, but if colour transparencies are available, put an editorial footnote on the press release and the caption so that the pictures editor can ask for a photograph. If only colour is used, or might be wanted quickly, telephone first and offer the colour material.

10. On products or services, provide brochures and other explanatory material if the media are likely to find this helpful.

11. Some products or services really need to be sampled; examples include stage productions, films, recorded music, books, and so on, as well as new cars or holidays. A pre-release under an embargo to journalists who need to let you have their opinions of the product must be an essential element of news management of such products.

12. Use embargoes if the media are likely to need time to research a story or sample a product, but otherwise, try to avoid them.

13. If the story is of sufficient interest and one's credibility with the relevant journalists is high enough, advance warning can help to improve the likely coverage.

14. Quotes should be attributable to someone of authority who can be interviewed by the media if necessary.

15. Make sure that the story reaches the right media, and don't trust the post, especially at Christmas or at other public holidays, if the story is time-sensitive. Use couriers, facsimile machines and the wire services, especially those of Two-Ten Communications, the former UNS, if timing is tight.

16. Look for additional background material to offer the media, such as background articles or features, interview possibilities, photographic opportunities, recorded radio interviews or even interviews and background commentary on broadcast quality video tape for television stations – the so-called 'video news release' – if this is going to be helpful.

17. Ensure that there is a contact name on any material issued to the media, and that this includes an out-of-hours telephone number since many journalists are writing their stories at times when most of the population is not at work.

18. Try to avoid clashing with major announcements, not only by competitors, but in other fields as well, if these are likely to dominate the media. A major company news story can be swamped, and even sunk without trace, by a major political event, an international crisis or natural disaster.

19. Functions or events, no matter how important, should always be covered by the organization's own specially commissioned photographer there, just in case the newspaper photographers don't turn up. The commissioned photographer must be someone able to provide prints or transparencies quickly enough to be of use to the newspapers. This point should be borne in mind no matter how significant the event or how good the organization's media credibility. The Wright brothers have already been mentioned, and we do well to remember that example. Never take anything for granted!

20. Be aware of issues which are likely to affect the organization

and ensure that management has a considered official reaction which can be given to the media and other interested parties, such as pressure groups and politicians. The press office must be aware of the official line on such matters, while they should have the support of specialists, if necessary, and directors or senior management must be able to speak directly to the media if interviews are required.

21. Finally, remember that a photograph really is worth a thousand words, if it is a good one, and more especially if it is different. Products are meant to be used, and should be shown at work, and if it makes sense, put people into the photographs using the products, providing scale and additional interest.

Index